Leading in Tough Times

The Manager's Guide to Responsibility, Trust, and Motivation

Richard S. Deems, Ph.D.
Terri A. Deems, Ph.D.

HRD Press • Amherst • Massachusetts

Published by:
Human Resource Development Press, Inc.
22 Amherst Road
Amherst, MA 01002
(800) 822-2801 (U.S. and Canada)
(413) 253-3488
(413) 253-3490 (fax)
http://www.hrdpress.com

ISBN 0-87425-722-0

Production services by Jean Miller
Editorial services by Sally Farnham
Cover design by Eileen Klockars

Acknowledgements

Many people have had input into this book—and are we ever grateful! First, there are all the people who so generously shared their insight, time, and energy for interviews. It is gratifying to find leaders who are willing to take time from hectic schedules to talk about leading in tough times. And there were many others who contributed their time, energy, and thoughts as well. We want to thank you all for your excellent contributions!

Aldonna R. Ambler, CMC, CSP; Ambler Growth Strategy Consultants, Inc.; Melanie K. Arntsen, Ph.D., Xamicus; Marty Baddeloo, Solutions Kept Simple; Herb Baum, The Dial Corporation; Charles D. Goldman, Atty., Washington, D.C.; Natalie Jenkins, VP & Director of Sales, Innova Training & Consulting, Inc.; Steve Kastendieck, McKesson Medication Management; Betsy McKnight Latko, Deems McKnight Latko Associates, Inc.; Phyllis Lepke, ISU Foundation; Jim Lewis, president, Relationship Marketing, Inc.; Gail McDonald, Transition Resources, Inc.; Todd McDonald, ATW Training & Consulting; Mel Rambo, National Travelers Life; Vally M. Sharpe, M.A., Solutions for Organizational Success; David Slaughter, Slaughter and Associates, Inc.; Pete Taggart, Solutions for Business; Rudy Uribe, Core Training Systems; Tom Van Fossen, Met Life; Mary Westheimer, BookZone.com.

Second, there are our own mentors—people who have helped shape our thoughts, ideas, experiences, and approaches to leadership. We thank you deeply.

Third, there are our family members: They not only gave up family time, but also read manuscripts, made suggestions, shared stories, and encouraged us to get this done on schedule. Special thanks to executive coach Sandra Brownfield Deems; retired insurance executive brother Robert Deems; and the kids, Annie and Ben Laswell.

Finally, we thank each other. Terri has made her dad stretch. Dad has helped Terri keep her feet on the ground. We might even try to write another book together. Hey, we said "might."

Table of Contents

Preface

Think about the several crises we've seen during 2001 and 2002 here in the United States: the great "dot com bust" and a stuttering economy; massive layoffs; the tragedies of September 11; corporate blowouts and handcuffed CEOs. Unemployment is up and morale is down. For many of today's leaders, this is the first time they have ever had to deal with hard times—economic slowdown, recession, natural disaster, terrorism. These are indeed tough times in which to be a leader.

The July 2002 issue of *Fast Company* quotes Nissan president and CEO Carlos Ghosn as saying, "If you ask people to go through a difficult period of time, they have to trust that you're sharing it with them." That's a good way to think about this book—how to lead in ways that show people that you really are "there" with them.

What does it take to successfully lead during tough times? As Ghosn and many others have shown us, it takes acting responsibly, living so people trust you, and knowing how to lead so that people stay motivated and don't lose hope. These aren't qualities reserved just for tough times, however. Leadership in tough times is the same as it is in good.

What is different, when times are tough, is how conscious we are of our actions: a more mindful attitude toward our work, our workplaces, and the people who work there. It's awareness, for example, that the day after announcing the big downsizing is not the best time to show up in a new BMW. It's the knowledge that denial and retreat won't make bad things disappear.

As you read this book, you may even be relieved to learn that being a leader doesn't mean you must also be a hero. The days of looking at corporate CEOs as some kind of heroic figurehead are gone. People are tired of hype and spin and more interested in working with someone who is genuine, who is present in good times and bad, and who is connected with the work and with the people at work. They want leaders who make decisions and take action based on something other than self-interest.

In the following pages, we'll talk with you about how to be a strong, connected presence in the midst of tough times. But let's start with a basic understanding. We are working in this book from the belief that our readers already have a sound knowledge of basic business principles.

Our focus here is *not* to give you a quick refresher course in basic business practices. Rather, our intention is to look beyond the numbers to those actions that will most help you, your organization, and the people who work with you survive and even thrive in the midst of difficult times.

We don't think you'll find many surprises here. As Ray Jackson, associate dean of the leadership school at Unisys University, describes, "Leadership in bad times is basically the same as it is in good times." Or it should be. Many leaders believe, in fact, that it's easier being a good leader in hard times than to be a good leader in good times. Jim Lewis, president of Relationship Marketing, Inc., reminds us, "If we thought as deeply about the issues when the times are good, many of our issues when times are bad are lessened."

What may be the real challenge during tough times, though, is maintaining your own confidence and courage as a leader. We don't want to give you a one-size-fits-all "how-to" manual. Rather, we hope this book will help shore up your confidence and courage by affirming what the best leaders already know, and by giving you examples, stories, and activities you can use to take confident steps.

This book is divided into two sections. The first, "Principles to Lead By," explores seven principles that guide the actions of people who have excelled during difficult times. Though these principles are discussed individually, you will see that they are closely intertwined. The second section, "Leadership in Action," explores specific examples of tough times and how others have used those principles to bring about meaningful and sustainable change.

Many of the principles describe actions that some often think of as "soft skills." While it is true that these qualities are not going to find a place on your accounting spreadsheet, don't be fooled into believing there is anything "soft" about them. They are as critical to your success during your own "tough times" as your marketing, hiring, or accounting practices. Surviving and thriving during difficult times starts with your own mindset, your attitudes, and shifting your thinking from *How?,* to *What matters,* and *Why?*

Finally, you will see that the activities in this book are meant to be completed by either an individual leader or a work group or team. It is our desire to not only pose ideas, questions, and challenges to an individual reader, but to encourage dialogue about topics people might not typically discuss. We hope you'll use it in that spirit. Share your own conclusions with others you work with, and really listen to theirs. This is how you build a worklife where people truly work together in a spirit of creativity, community, and purpose.

We hope you enjoy the book and find it helpful. Feel free to contact us about the topics in this book. We may be reached at 515-964-0219 or by email at vitalwork@aol.com.

Richard S. Deems, Ph.D., and Terri A. Deems, Ph.D.

Section One: Principles to Lead By . . .

"Problems cannot be solved
at the same level of consciousness
that created them."
(Albert Einstein)

Chapter One: Lead the Way

"It is our own transformation that creates the best climate for change."
(Peter Block, ***The Answer to How Is Yes***)

One of the positive aspects of a crisis is that it forces people to rethink their behavior.

Many of us grew up hearing "actions speak louder than words." Nowhere is it more evident than in the workplace, especially during 120tough times. It doesn't matter if you are CEO of a huge conglomerate or leader of a small project team, people will look to you as their example. As leader, you must have the courage to live your values and model the behavior you want to see in your organization. This is how you lead the way.

During tough times, your intentional modeling is vital to help focus people's attention, energy, and effort. As a leader, you create the climate for change, just as you create the climate for community, innovation, and ownership. Or you're creating the climate to make change unlikely. The old saying holds true: If you're not part of the solution, then you're part of the problem.

Here are seven actions you can take to set an example for others and lead the way in tough times.

1. Step Up

Leaders must be present and visible. Withdrawing or staying quiet is the wrong thing to do. A crisis or major event gives you, the leader, a chance to be heard and judged in ways that the good times simply do not provide.

Relationship Marketing, Inc., president Jim Lewis describes a critical decision following the tragedies of 9/11. "We had our annual Tailgate party scheduled for the 13th of September. After 9/11, many people advised that we cancel the party." Celebrating after such catastrophic events seemed cold and unfeeling. But the values that Jim often stressed included working and playing together, celebrating spirit, and meeting challenges in a unified way. "To me, this was a key time for us to come together and celebrate the American spirit that got us through many formidable challenges in the past and will do the same in the future." People need to be assured that those in charge are confident. "Going ahead with the Tailgate was the best thing we could have done." Was it an emotional gathering? Of course. "But it somehow gave us all added confidence, knowing we were OK, and gave us a chance to honor those who had made the ultimate sacrifice."

Stepping up means that you make difficult decisions with confidence; that you keep yourself in the public eye within your organization and your community; and that you make your values tangible, even when others disagree with you. People look for leaders to step up, especially during difficult times, to stand with courage for what they believe in. There will be times when you pay a high price for it, because living our values can also mean swimming against the tide. But you do it, regardless.

2. Know Yourself

Being an example and leading the way demands that you become more self-aware. Knowing ourselves is one of the most difficult tasks we face. But until we really know our strengths and weaknesses, our desires, our motivations, our intentions, and our values—and explore the consistency of our actions—we won't succeed in any meaningful way. We will not have the respect we need to lead others. We will not have the consistency needed to be seen as credible and trustworthy. And we will not have the confidence necessary to thrive in tough times.

Know Your Intentions. Knowing yourself begins with knowing your intentions or motives—knowing what matters to you, knowing which values will guide your actions, and knowing what you are willing to commit to. This isn't a one-time, sit-down-and-think-about-it activity. It needs to be an ongoing process you commit to. Sure it will take time, but make personal reflection a priority, as much as evaluating your market presence or exploring new work processes to enhance performance.

Set aside your organization for right now. Why? Because it's often too easy to simply let our organizations tell us what we should commit to. Instead, take out a piece of paper and write down your values, motives, or intentions. Consider questions like these:

- What is worth doing?
- Am I doing what I truly want to be doing?
- What is it I really want to create in my life?
- What stops me from being everything I could be? And what actions do I need to take to remove those obstacles?

- If I got what I want, what would I have? What is my true purpose?

Intentions hold little meaning, however, unless they drive our actions in a real way. Take the above exercise a step further. Take out your calendar or appointment book and look over what you've done this past month.

- How do your actions compare with your intentions?
- How much of your time is spent doing the things that you've said are worth doing?
- What inconsistencies do you see between what you say (espoused values) and what you do (values-in-action)?
- On what kind of activities are you spending your greatest amount of time?
- Where are you spending the least amount of time?

Challenge Your Assumptions. Knowing yourself demands that you not only make time to examine your behavior, but also your mindsets and your assumptions. We all have assumptions we make about other people or how the world works. Challenge these. For example, there are three major beliefs that tend to guide our work, all involving this idea that we can (and should) somehow "motivate" people toward certain ends. The assumption here is that people need some kind of external stimulus in order to give their best to an organization's goals. From such assumptions grow the following beliefs:

- It's part of human nature to pursue self-interest.
- People do what they are rewarded for.
- If something doesn't get measured, it doesn't get done.

Consider how alternative assumptions would change your work. Suppose it's not your job to motivate—that you'll cease using your approval and possibility of advancement as a carrot for certain performance. All carrots will be banned, in fact. Suppose that people are naturally motivated to work toward a meaningful, common vision. When we fail to see motivated people, our questions would have to change from "How do I motivate them?" to "What is getting in the way of their motivation?" This changes the conversation considerably.

What are your assumptions about work and about people at work? Are these assumptions really accurate, or simply beliefs you have picked up along the way from other people? Make your assumptions clear, and then challenge them. You might be surprised at just how well this frees you up to see new options.

Know What You Do Best. Most of us can spend a great deal of time and energy doing things that we simply don't do all that well. Knowing what you really do best, and devoting your time and energies to these things, will simplify your life immensely. For example, Richard knew that what he really did best was to innovate, to start new projects, and to cultivate support for new ideas. But he spent very little time doing these things—instead he was spending a great deal of energy trying to organize himself, maintain an office efficiently, and keep track of necessary information. He was stressed and not able to focus on what he really enjoyed doing. His performance suffered, and burnout was imminent.

The solution was simple: find someone who had a knack for the things Richard didn't do well. Richard took the time to figure out what he really did best and most enjoyed doing, and turned everything else over to people who liked doing what Richard didn't. Richard's stress dropped. His performance improved. Work was a good place to be again.

What do you do best and most enjoy doing? Take a hard, honest look at yourself. If you're not sure, ask other people for their input. Conduct a 360-degree feedback on yourself. Write down your responsibilities and accomplishments, then go back through and mark the ones that really gave you most pleasure. Before you're halfway through, we believe you'll see a pattern emerging—certain kinds of activities that you thrive on, and activities that you simply don't do well. Then, find ways to turn those "don't do well" activities over to someone else.

It's unrealistic to believe that we can do everything well. This is the reason behind the need to "hire smarter" than you.

Our strength lies in knowing who we are, what we stand for, and what we do best. People are more likely to reflect on their own behavior as a result of seeing our self-reflection. By examining our actions, mindsets, and natural strengths, we are more likely to take actions that result in meaningful change. Complete Activity 1-1 to help examine your strengths and weaknesses.

Activity 1-1. Examining Your Strengths and Weaknesses

What do I really do best and most enjoy doing?

____
____
____
____
____
____
____

These are the things that I have trouble with:

____
____
____
____
____
____
____
____

Here are people who do these things very well, who I can turn to:

____
____
____
____
____
____
____
____

Encourage the people you work with to take a reflective approach to their work as well. In the midst of daily activities, take time to pause and ask yourself and others: Are we really doing what is most important to do? Are we creating a world we want to live in (the world of your community, organization, department, or work unit)? Are we doing something that matters? Who are we, and what do we wish to become?

3. Realize That You May Be the Problem

This is one of the toughest mindsets to crack—the realization that we, ourselves, might be the problem, or at least part of the problem. We create our own chains—mental chains that cause us to filter and limit what we hear, what we see, and what we understand. We become the "victims" of circumstances.

We live in a culture that often seems to value a victim mindset. For example, when we didn't get the order, it's *the customer* who couldn't see the benefits of our product. When the change didn't work in our organization, it was because *the employees* were resisting. When we didn't get the promotion, it's because *"they"* just didn't see how valuable we are. When we lost the account, it's because *the competitor* didn't play fair. It's the employees. The board. The customers. The competition. The government. The economy.

Remember that people will follow your lead. Any willingness on your part to play victim leads everyone else to play victim as well—to blame the always present "they" for missed goals or poor performance.

We can be so intent on promoting what we believe that we don't listen to others or hear what is really being said. We ask the easy questions rather than the right ones. We focus on ways to get "them" to change. Our energies would be better placed if we stopped worrying about what's wrong with "them" and see what can be changed in ourselves—our perspectives, attitudes, beliefs.

The next time you hear yourself saying or thinking that the fault lies with "them," stop yourself. You are the leader. The model. The example. Be one. You can do absolutely nothing about "them." You can do everything about yourself.

Leading the way means you begin understanding the problem and exploring solutions locally first—you start with yourself. When your employees see your willingness to start with yourself, they will be much more open to examining and changing their own behaviors as well.

It's all about learning:

- Leading is learning. Let go of your comfort zones; try new things, think in new ways, challenge yourself. Learning is about doing, not knowing.
- Let go of your control. Don't focus on what you must give up; focus on what you may gain. Remember that you'll never get to second base with your foot still on first.
- Think of mistakes as great feedback mechanisms. If nothing else, they tell us "where the gold isn't" and trigger learning.
- Encourage others to challenge your decisions. Be willing to be disturbed, to have your beliefs and ideas challenged by what others think. This is how we grow.

4. Lead with a Human Face

Omar Aktouf coined the phrase "leading with a human face." To us this means leading in an authentic and genuine way. When people are polled about what employees want in a leader, the words "authentic" and "genuine" always come up. Leaders often believe they must maintain a heroic presence of some sort—be super-human. But in reality, people don't need some kind of gung-ho god. "People are looking for reassuring, everyday leadership," says Ray Jackson, dean of the leadership school at Unisys University. "People want that person to be real, somebody they can count on, somebody that will be there."

Be Fully Alive. People want a leader who leads in a human way; someone who is fully alive. When someone leads in a human way, they are also recognizing the humanness in others. Seems like that would be a natural, doesn't it? And yet we're surrounded by examples of leaders who seem to think they and all the rest of us are automatons—objects to be acted upon. Any expression of emotion or independent thinking is repressed. If you're not willing to work 12- or 15-hour days, you're not a team player. Check your soul at the door on Monday, and pick it up again at the end of the week.

The leader who is fully alive, however, recognizes that human life is emotional as well as objective; it's dynamic and often full of contradictions. And that life involves more than your organization. Being fully alive as a leader means you are free to be expressive—to express joy and sadness, excitement and frustration, confidence and uncertainty. You work with a sense of fun—that deep sense of enjoyment and pleasure that comes from working as if what you do and the people around you do indeed matter. Being fully alive means that you are not always certain, but you are willing to take a chance. It means things like speaking the truth and seeking it in others. It means working from the heart.

Live a Balanced Life. Our work should be in the service of our lives, rather than the other way around. There is a tremendous amount of talk today of people wanting more balance in their lives. We often find our life and our work in opposition to each other, as if they were two separate things. And many of our organizations contribute to this idea by encouraging 60- and 70-hour work weeks. As one IT manager described, "It's like, when I'm not working, it's my life, but when I am working, it's someone else's." This life-split puts us off balance: Should we engage in what has meaning for us, or simply do things that are useful and practical and that have an instrumental purpose in our lives?

Leading with a human face is about being in balance wherever we are, whether at the office or out fishing with the kids. And we must encourage balance in others. At Great Harvest Bread, people can be fired for regularly working more than 40 hours a week. People there work hard to live a full and balanced life, one that allows them to wake up in the morning refreshed and excited about what the day might bring. The key is to decide what's important in each person's life, then design and conduct your work in a way that supports that end.

Treat People as People. Just as we increasingly focus our lives on instrumental purposes, we also have a tendency to use people as instruments. Too often, we see other people's value simply in terms of what they can do for us. We have created a culture that assigns value based on how effective something is, how much leverage it can give us, or what return we receive on our investment.

It's a pattern spread throughout our culture and has become so common that we hardly notice it anymore. Land that cannot be built on, worked, or drilled into is worthless because land without commerce has no value. Colleges used to be in the business of wisdom and building knowledge; today it's building resumes. In fact, we see education in general as being a way to prepare for a career, rather than a way to prepare to participate fully in one's society. Home décor is organized around workspaces. Dining rooms become offices. Our car, a restaurant. Organizational productivity depends on reducing human costs. We reward organizations that minimize their need for people, relocate for lower wages, and consider safety and environmental restraints as excessive government regulation.

Treating people as people calls us to look beyond instrumental purpose and company asset. It means recognizing in a real and meaningful way that the members of our organizations are human, with all their human aspirations and foibles. We make mistakes and can learn from them.

Bring your true and best self into the world.

5. Make Use of Your Internal Expertise

Hard as it may be to believe, there really is nothing wrong with telling employees that you don't know everything. You're not supposed to know everything. That's why you hire great people. So make use of your internal expertise. No one knows more about how things work, what will result in greater quality or performance, or ways to reduce costs than the people who do the work.

Help people feel powerful. Strengthen them. There is a lot of talk in organizations about empowerment. But that's mostly all we get—the talk. More times than not, empowerment is just another buzzword and has little to do with fundamental change in the division of power, profits, and authority. And yet, we know that if our organizations are to truly thrive during the tough times, we absolutely must help people to feel powerful in a real way.

Give people the control and influence necessary to do whatever it takes to get the job done. Increase their power by helping them build their skills and knowledge, and by making sure they have the resources they need to be successful. Make them creators of their own destiny. Take the time to regularly talk with people, informally, on the job, to learn what it is that will help them be most effective. Then see that they have it.

During the tough times, you want people to have a strong sense of organizational citizenship. You want it. Your people want it, too. Help them to know this is their place to create.

Do what you do best, and give the rest to someone else.

6. Character Matters

Remember that people are watching you—and they have a choice about where they work, even in a soft job market. Character still matters. As a leader in tough times, you need to conduct yourself in a way that shows you know this.

Scott McNealy, of Sun Microsystems, Inc., described in a recent interview, "During tough times, you don't beat on people. You have the same team you had when the company was growing at 60% a year. They didn't suddenly turn stupid or lazy." Instead, in tough times "I'm cheerleading. I'm telling people how great they're doing." It's during the good times that he gets out the whip to prevent people from getting complacent, arrogant, or sloppy.

What shows your character? For Relationship Marketing's Jim Lewis, it's about working with integrity and consistent values: "Practice what you preach. Always, always go to your governing values and make sure you are doing what you said you would do." Compassion for others is also critical to Lewis. "But don't expect to receive credit for compassion. It's important you make decisions for the right reasons and not simply for getting credit for being compassionate or understanding. That's self-serving. If you need recognition for your compassion, you're not a leader."

In *Flight of the Buffalo*, authors Belasco and Stayer write, "it's the right action that matters most." Only take actions that can be defended and believed under harsh public scrutiny. Take this simple test: Think about your actions and words today. If they were to be discussed in tomorrow's *Wall Street Journal*, how would you feel? If you believe that character still counts, and that your actions must be consistent with your values, then what you see in tomorrow's paper should be a source of pride rather than one of shame.

You don't have to do things because they are the most efficient, increase productivity, or will result in the greatest financial return. You can do something simply because it is the right thing to do.

7. Be the Change

Mahatma Gandhi challenged us in many ways to view our world differently. Among his most powerful sayings was this: "You must be the change you wish to see in the world."

Absolutely nothing will have greater impact on your employees than your own actions—your ability to "be the change." A rousing speech can fire the imagination and spur people to short-term action, but it is your example that will really make the difference. If you want people to approach their work thoughtfully, then be a reflective person. If you want people to work with a sense of joy and pride, then take joy and pride in all that you do. If you want people to embrace change and work from the heart, they must see you doing so as well.

What change do you want to see in your organization? Reduced costs? Improved quality? Greater innovation? Faster turnaround? If you want more open communication, don't hide in your office. If you want more creative thinking, then work from possibility rather than from what the competition is doing.

Be the change. People admire and follow leaders who are able to make visions and values real and tangible. People will watch you for cues for their own commitment, their energy, and their ethics. Are you doing what matters? Are you creating a world you really want to live in?

Review

This chapter has been more about thinking and reflection than about taking specific actions. That's because when you lead during tough times, you must become very conscious of your motives, intentions, beliefs, and attitudes toward others. As you become more aware of what really drives and matters to you, your actions will take on a new focus and energy. Remember:

- *Step up*. People need to hear what you believe and then see it in action.
- *Know yourself.* This is the only way you can be sure you are acting on, rather than simply reacting to, the world around you.
- *Consider that you may be part of the problem*. Examine your mindsets as well as your actions to be sure you are really part of the solution.
- *Lead with a human face*. Authentic leadership trumps spin every time.
- *Use your internal expertise*. You might be surprised at just how bright your own people are.
- *Your character matters*. Take pride in that.
- *Be the change*. Change happens one person at a time, starting with you.

It's not easy leading in tough times. But you can do it!

Chapter Two: Connecting with Others

"Good leaders make people feel that they're at the very heart of things, not at the periphery."
(Warren Bennis)

We keep an old sign up on our office wall. Many of you have probably seen one like it. The sign helps us remember that communication is key, even when it involves a difficult subject: "Sure, we know that communication is a problem here, but we're not going to discuss it with the employees."

Sadly, this kind of thinking is alive and well in America's workplaces. A few years ago a company called us in to help them work through some morale issues within an account sales department. Turnover had been steadily increasing, and people in general just didn't seem to be happy at work. The department was facing a significant reorganization, and leaders decided that now was a good time to dig in to some of their "people issues." Conversations with people identified that trust was a major problem. People believed there was lots of secrecy and hidden agendas around them. When asked if they ever discussed this with their managers, several people responded: "No, there are some things we just don't talk about around here."

Among other recommendations that we made, we suggested managers and teams spend some time really digging in to this sense of secrecy and lack of trust. In a meeting with some of their top leaders, we asked them to share our report with the members of the department and to begin talking about the things "we don't talk about here." After listening to us and nodding their heads, the leaders made the decision to keep the report to themselves. As one described, "Why bring this out in the open? It's really too sensitive and emotional an issue to talk about." As if it weren't being talked about already!

We connect with other people through our communication—the transference and understanding of meaning. We're communicating constantly, whether we are aware of it or not, through our words, tone of voice, body movements, even our silences. We've done it all our lives. You'd think we'd be good at it, wouldn't you?

Yet every day in our organizations we see the effects of poor talking, listening, and information-sharing habits. To counteract poor communication, we train on communication skills, build policies around it, and create charts and graphs to try to manage it. Yet even after decades of research and study and writing and coaching and hammering on this topic, communication still ranks right at the top of major workplace issues identified by employees.

Good communication is essential for any group's effectiveness, whether that group is a small work unit, a family, a community, a baseball team, or an organization. During the tough times, communication can make or break your organization. Misunderstanding, lack of communication, single-loop feedback, no feedback, language and meaning ambiguities all can have results ranging from the mildly frustrating and uncomfortable to catastrophic and deadly. This chapter will not attempt to cover all aspects of communication; after all, communication is a vast field of study, far exceeding the boundaries of this book. What we can do, though, is examine some of the basis for poor communication and consider several guidelines to boost your communication performance.

Basis for Poor Communication

Why is poor communication so epidemic in our organizations? Organizational communication is often treated as something tangible, something we can actually see, touch, and hold. So we try to manage it and control it. It's easy to fool ourselves into overlooking its unpredictability. Remember that childhood telephone game and how much fun it was to hear how twisted the message was by the time it reached the last person? It's not so funny when it's happening within your organization.

While training and communication policies can help improve communication, they will not be enough to ensure effective communication practices. Why? Here are four of the biggest factors that come into play.

Individual Differences

We each tend to believe that we communicate well. After all, we communicate the way *we* think is appropriate, don't we? We don't stop to consider—or ask—whether others find our communication adequate or not. We forget about the role of individual differences.

For example, Richard can believe he is telling Sandie all she needs to know about a scheduling change—when and what it will be, and who it will involve. Sandie, though, gets frustrated because Richard is leaving out what she believes is key information—the reason for the change. Richard is irritated because Sandie seems to be ignoring or resisting what he has told her. Sandie's angry because Richard is, "as usual," withholding information. What has happened is that both Richard and Sandie are filtering or making sense of the message through their own personal way of acting on the world. And these ways are different for each of us.

Selective Perception and Information Overload

Every day, we are bombarded by thousands of pieces of information: phone calls, e-mail, reports, hallway conversations, meetings, newspapers and television, to say nothing of the information we receive almost unconsciously from observations of everything around us.

Humans have only a limited capacity to process information, so we must somehow sift through all the information we receive. We sort and select, ignore, and forget information, while actively processing and assimilating other data.

Defensiveness

Communication is further complicated when we add emotion into the equation. Defensiveness, in particular, will muddy the communication waters; if we're feeling somehow threatened, our tendency is for fight-or-flight. We react in ways that reduce our ability to effectively transmit and understand meanings. In this age of information, we also equate information with power. And we look at it as yet another zero-sum game—giving power to others will somehow reduce my own. So we defend what we have; we withdraw, withhold, protect. Vital communication processes such as wide information sharing and feedback loops can become restricted.

Language and Meaning Differences

We all know that words mean different things to different people. And still we act as though our meaning is everyone's meaning. A manager we once worked with was frustrated because a worker simply wasn't performing to the level needed. "I kept telling Jim, make sure your time is spent effectively, that your actions are effective. He just seems to ignore me." He didn't consider that his sense of "effective" and Jim's could be two very different things.

Meanings are in us, not simply in our words. As our organizations become increasingly diverse in terms of age, cultural background, educational experience, and in many other ways, we have increasing differences in our word use, speech patterns, and meanings.

Key Communication Strategies

There are many different ways to communicate effectively with people at work. We won't try to cover everything here. Among the most important, though, are connecting with people at work and being visible and involved. Take a moment and think about your own communication strategies:

- How are you most likely to communicate with your managers, officers, or other designated leaders?
- How are you most likely to communicate with other employees?
- What methods do you use to regularly "take the pulse" of your organization in terms of mood, climate, and morale?
- How do you gather ideas from people, find out what is bothering them, or learn ways to help people be more effective in their jobs?
- What methods do you use to share "painful" information with your people?

Communication is essential for leading in tough times. Here are two examples of CEOs who know how to communicate with their people.

Connecting with Others

Communication is about connecting with others, in simple and direct ways. Take "Hot Dogs with Herb," for example. Employees grab a hot dog, add mustard and relish, and sit down for lunch with Herb Baum, CEO and chair of The Dial Corporation. Agenda? "I like to know what's on the minds of the people who work here," Baum states.

"It's a way of keeping in touch with your people," Baum adds, "and I've been doing lunches in one way or another my entire career." How did "Hot Dogs with Herb" come about? "I was raised in Chicago," he describes, "home of some great hot dogs. Growing up, it was my favorite food. Sometimes it was my only food."

"Hot Dogs with Herb" started soon after Baum took over as president, chairman, and CEO of The Dial Corporation. He had been on the board of directors for several years. When Dial's earnings continued to slip, the other board members moved him into the number one position. "One of the best moves we've ever made," adds more than one director.

"I know that leaders need to know what is on the minds of their people, and this is one of the best ways I could do it," Baum believes. "Sure, you can do a paper and pencil survey, but this way I get the real mood of the people, in words they use. It helps me know how to plan and what we need to do to make people happy. Without happy people," Baum says, "there's no real quality, no real productivity, no chance for cutting edge products and services."

Herb regularly invites a group of employees to have hot dogs with him. Once he's had lunch with all the employees, he starts over again.

And it's working. In the past two years, The Dial Corporation has turned weak performance into banner results and added almost $1 billion in market cap to the company and stockholders. While many of the stocks of Dial's peers declined in value, Dial's stock increased.

Employees like working at Dial. They work hard. Performance is high. Pride in the company is high. Innovation is high. And it all started with direct communication from the top, around a table with a hot dog in your hand.

Here are Baum's four guidelines for communicating.

1. *Always keep all of your employees in the communication loop.* You can do it through e-mails, newsletters, or in-house cable. They deserve to know what's going on within the organization.

2. *Never let them hear news about the company from the media first.* All employees must hear it from their leaders first. You do this with company-wide meetings, or small-group meetings, and sometimes even with hot dogs.

3. *Always tell the truth.* Then you don't have to worry about what you said to one person and what you said to someone else. People need to trust their leaders. "It's essential in these times," Baum adds.

4. *Communication has to be frequent.* You can't have just one company lunch a year. Communication from the top has to be ongoing. People need to know they can come to your office and get an immediate hearing.

Visibility and Involvement

Connecting with others is also about high visibility and involvement. When it was announced that Mel Rambo would be taking over as president of National Travelers Life (NTL), the employees gave him a standing ovation. As chief actuary at NTL, Rambo knew the people and knew the insurance business inside and out. He also knew he had lots of work to do. The company was losing money, and to salvage it, a big chunk of its book of business was being sold. Without the business, there wasn't need for half the workforce.

"During this whole time," Rambo learned, "communication was essential. The more we talked with employees about what was going to happen, or what might happen, the less tension there seemed to be among the people." Division leaders held regular meetings to keep their people informed on decisions that might affect them.

"The full company meetings were the most important," Rambo believes. "We held several with all of our employees in the same room at the same time. Everyone received the same information from the same person. The rumor mill was still going, but at least everybody had the same information."

Other popular communication actions Rambo took, according to several employees, involved eating lunch in the cafeteria, keeping his office door open, and walking around the building talking to people several times a day. People could stop Mel and ask him any question they wanted. If they didn't want others to overhear the conversation, they knew they could find Rambo in his office early in the morning. "This kind of communication affirmed that nothing drastic was going to be thrown to us at the last minute," one employee stated.

National Travelers Life is showing a profit within the first year of Rambo's leadership. "I can't stress enough how important communication with all employees is," he affirms. "The other part of communication is having the open door policy, of being available and ready to talk with people who have questions."

Going into his new assignment, Rambo knew how important communication would be. "I tried as hard as I could to make sure that no one heard anything first from outside the company, and I always let people know they could ask me anything they wanted whenever they saw me." Then he made sure that his door was open. People would see him several times a day, which made them feel, as long as Mel wasn't hiding in his corner, things would be OK.

Everyday Communication

Tough times can make everyday communication difficult. Leaders often become so involved in trying to run the company, it can look as if they're hiding even when they're not. Look hard to find ways to be visible and easily accessible to others.

Remember, too, that accessibility is not just about people having access to the leaders, but having access to information as well. This is the only way to fully encourage people's involvement. For years, companies have shown that open book management—where people have full access to the same information that leaders have—is a critical part of the highest performing organizations. It reduces any sense of secrecy and hidden agendas. It helps all employees develop their business literacy. And it helps build employee commitment and ownership of the organization.

During tough times, you want people who are committed, trusting, knowledgeable of the business, and aware of what's going on. Business consultant Marty Baddeloo describes it this way: "I think of a company like a sports team. In baseball, you don't tell your batter to bunt without also signaling to the runner on first that it's going to happen." He continues, "A business should operate the same way. Let your players know what is happening, let them know their role, the expectations, and the overall game plan. And let them know if that game plan has to change. Keeping people informed and those communication channels open is critical."

Simple, everyday conversation keeps you visible and keeps those communication channels open. Common guidelines for talking with others include:

1. Clearly state your opinion, idea, or need. Help your listeners focus by beginning with statements like, "I suggest that…" "Thinking out loud, I…" "Consider…" "This is what I mean…" or "Here is what I believe…"

2. Describe how you arrived at your reasoning. Begin with statements like, "Here's how I got there…" "The reasons for my thinking are…" "I decided this because…"

3. Use specific examples. Clarify with statements like, "To illustrate this…" or "Here is an example of what I mean…"

4. Make your assumptions known. Make statements beginning with, "The assumptions underlying my belief are…" "I assume that…" "This is my experience…"

5. Ask about other people's views. Involve the other people by asking, "How do you see this situation?" "What are your concerns about my views?" "Can you give me an example?" "How did you arrive at that?"

6. Seek alternative views. Ask questions like, "What is your reaction?" "How could I look at this situation differently?" "Do you see any gaps in my thinking?" "What might I have missed?"

7. Encourage people to challenge your ideas or assumptions. Ask questions like, "What contrary evidence is there?" "Do you see things differently?" "What is it about what I'm saying that raises doubts for you?" "Does my thinking seem valid to you?"

8. Listen. Practice active listening skills. Focus your attention on what the other person is saying, rather than on what you want to say next. Clear your mind of distractions. Restate the other person's key points to be sure you understood correctly.

Listening and Feedback

Both Herb's and Mel's stories underline the importance of close interaction, being visible, and actively encouraging communication and information sharing. They also underline the importance of an often-overlooked aspect of communication: listening.

Listening is more than simple auditory reception. Our meanings and messages come in many forms—words, symbols, feelings, physical reactions, and so on. The key to good listening, as Herb and Mel both show us, lies in being receptive to messages and outwardly inviting feedback.

Choose Your Channel

As leaders we are surrounded by different choices for communicating. Do we use the phone? E-mail? Memo? Board meeting? Lunch? Typically, the channel we use depends on how clear or ambiguous, routine or nonroutine, our message is. Clear, routine messages that do not require immediate feedback are effectively communicated through one-way media, such as voice mail or written memo. During tough times, however, our messages are rarely routine and clear. Anxiety can tempt us to use impersonal, one-way communication channels. But tough times call for a richer channel that allows for the maximum of information to be conveyed, rapid feedback (verbal and nonverbal), and a personal touch. Face-to-face talk provides the richest channel. See Figure 2-1 for the hierarchy of channel richness.

Whenever possible, communicate directly. At Relationship Marketing, Inc., company president Jim Lewis describes, "You've got to communicate your message directly—don't rely on others to do it. Be confident enough to get in front of the troops. If you don't, it will backfire 9 times out of 10."

Figure 2-1. Hierarchy of Channel Richness

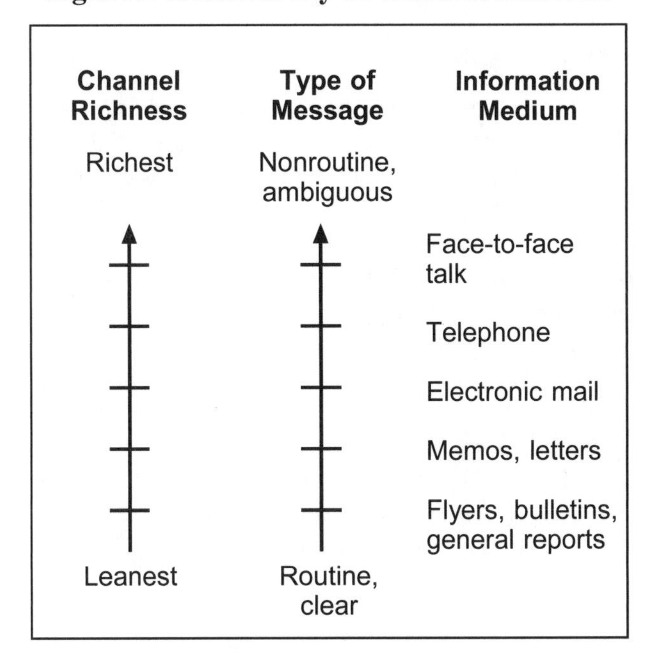

Hierarchy of Channel Richness from *Organizational Behavior,* Stephen P. Robbins

Communicate Through Action

We hear it all the time, "It's not what you say, it's what you do." But how easy it is to forget that, for most of us, our actions really do speak louder than our words! Within our organizations, leaders are role models. If there is an inconsistency between their words and their actions, people tend to give greater weight to the actions.

This can be a particularly powerful dynamic when it comes to ethics within the workplace. People can hear all day about the need for honesty, truth, and integrity, but if they see their leaders engaging in unethical behavior, they'll focus most on the behavior.

An interesting exception to this lies with the developing skill of putting "spin" on situations in a way that people put their faith in the words in spite of contradictory evidence and actions. But that's another book. What's important to remember here is that the most effective communication demands a very high level of consistency between our words and our actions.

Use a Mixed Media

People take in and process information differently. Some want to hear about the big picture and are annoyed with the details. Others want to see those details, right there in black and white. During tough times, it's important that people have trust and faith in you. As the leader, you help build this through open communication strategies. Use all the media available to you to communicate and interact with your people—communicate in person, in writing, using phone and e-mail, by drawing pictures, by creating a video.

When using a variety of media, you'll accommodate people's different learning styles, their natural ways of taking action, and even their generational differences. Phyllis Lepke, Iowa State University Foundation, describes, "There are generational differences in terms of information gathering. Learn what the strengths and weaknesses of each form of communication are and how they can be effectively used with the different generations."

Remember:

- Communicate directly, "Live!" and with confidence.
- Be direct and deal with the reality; employees and customers don't want excuses.
- Interact with your people, don't broadcast to them.
- Use rich communication channels.
- Share information widely and involve people throughout the organization.
- Seek input and feedback constantly—regularly take the pulse of the organization.

- Communicate in an authentic, genuine way; people usually know when they're receiving a snow job.
- Share the good, the bad, and the ugly. During difficult times, it's important that leaders deal with the reality and that the people at work know the stakes.
- Work to reduce rumor and fear through "extreme communication." Times of crisis spur rumors and fears. As leader, your job is to seek to lower that fear and reduce the chance of fear spurring other dysfunctional behavior.

Chapter Three: That Vision Thing

"There is no greater power for change than when a community discovers what it cares about."
(Margaret Wheatley, from ***The Four Directions***)

On August 28, 1963, Martin Luther King, Jr., delivered his "I Have a Dream" speech:

> *I say to you today, my friends, that in spite of the difficulties and frustrations of the moment I still have a dream. It is a dream deeply rooted in the American dream. I have a dream that one day this nation will rise up and live out the true meaning of its creed: We hold these truths to be self evident; that all men are created equal.*

King created a vision and invited America to join him in seeking that vision. The result? He moved a nation.

Visions are a powerful and vital part of leadership. They are the verbal description of an individual's or organization's focus—their desired state.

There are three critical questions that are fundamental to leading others, especially during the tough times. We used these recently in a class we conducted. Learners were preparing to create personal statements about their future and we put these questions up for them to consider:

1. What is the future we desire?
2. What do we believe in?
3. Why do we exist—why is it important for our organization to be alive and to thrive?

As the learners studied these questions, one manager remarked, "Oh yeah, here we go with that 'vision thing' again."

The word *vision* gets thrown around a lot nowadays—maybe too much. You can just about predict that it will be discussed in nearly any leadership book or article you will read. We don't know anyone who would say that vision and values were *not* important to the workplace.

Why, then, should we take time in *this* book to write about something that has been written about in so many excellent ways for years now?

The reason is this: During tough times, it is easy to set aside our vision as we get pulled in so many different directions—putting out fires, calming fears, dealing with the "hard" realities of business. There is a tendency in tough times to hunker down, protect, conserve, even withdraw. There's also a tendency to set aside "soft" things like purpose, caring, social responsibility, and any other big dreams we have for our organizations and our lives.

In our protective mode, it's easy to become narrowly obsessed with speed, numbers, efficiency, and technology. We're not saying that those things aren't important—of course they are. But they can lead us to lose sight of our focus. Without a focus, without our belief in a purpose larger than the organization itself, without a vision and the values that support it, the rest is pretty meaningless, isn't it?

Throughout history, both great and small organizations have survived and thrived during tough times with the help of a shared, compelling vision. Achieving this demands:

- Deep belief in the power of a vision
- Understanding of a vision's critical components
- Strong sense of personal vision
- Shared commitment within the organization
- Defining and focusing on what matters
- Living the stated values
- Beginning with the end in sight

The Power of Vision

For too many organizations, the word *vision* is tremendously overused. It's the name given to the fancy slogan the executives came up with and had carved on the brass plaque hanging in the reception area. It's a reason to head to a resort for three days to work on "that vision thing," play some golf, nod solemnly at each other, then return to the office amid great fanfare, usually followed by months of frustration as the creators ponder how to "get buy-in." There might be even more closed-door meetings where the leaders debate their mission, their values, their aspirations, and their purpose (as if there were any really good reason to distinguish between these).

That plaque on the wall isn't a vision. It's just a plaque on the wall.

Vision is the imagining of the future for the person, the family, the work unit, or the organization. It's the dream of you at your very best.

It's "fuzzier" than concrete management objectives, that's true, but it's often far more important. It answers our question, "What will success look like?" Without being able to answer that question, we're likely to get no further than where we are now.

Visions are inspiring. People at work want to make some money and earn a living, sure. But they also want to accomplish something that matters, to make a difference, and to achieve something no one else has achieved. And when people do that together—focusing their skills, talents, knowledge, and energies toward a common goal—tremendous things happen.

Yale University began a famous longitudinal study on goal-setting back in 1953. They surveyed the graduating class on Commencement Day to see who had written goals for what they wanted to do with their lives. Who had taken this step to define their focus? Only 3 percent had created this vision. Twenty years later, members of this class were surveyed once again. The 3 percent who had created a vision for themselves had achieved greater wealth than the other 97 percent combined. From this and many other similar studies since that time, we know the power of creating a clear goal for ourselves and committing to that goal in writing.

Vision is a standard you set for yourself that flows from a deep desire to do something meaningful, unique, and compelling. As Jack Hawley describes, "A grand and possible vision can bring a genuine sense of purpose, and that purpose feeds our craving for something bigger than ourselves."

Something "grand and possible." There's power in that. When leading during tough times, your vision provides the harness for that power.

Attributes of Vision

In organizations we use words like vision, mission, guiding principles, values, and purpose. Some people like to separate these or distinguish between them. We don't see any real value in doing that here. What you call it doesn't matter. We use the word *vision* here because of its familiarity and because of its etymology—to see.

What exactly is vision? Vision is our primary focus. It's what we organize ourselves around. What we strive for. It's what sets us apart from the others in our market. Kouzes and Posner describe it as "an ideal and unique image of the future." This is a definition similar to many others and one we find helpful to use in this discussion.

1. First, a vision *represents an ideal*. A vision assumes anything is possible. It implies a choice in what we value. Vision begins with dissatisfaction with the way things are and a desire for greater, more meaningful challenge. And it's about creating a new state of existence. Vision contains a firm belief that what can be imagined can become reality.
2. Vision also *sets us proudly apart* from others. It's unique to us and to what we value. Our vision expresses our purpose in the larger scheme of things—ourselves in the midst of others, our work unit within the organization, the organization within the world.
3. A third attribute of vision is the *emphasis on the future*. As a leader, you must be able to project yourself forward in time—anticipating, projecting, dreaming, and building. Our vision is our declaration not simply of where we're headed, but what we intend to create. Futurist John Schaar says it well: "The future is not some place we are going to, but one we are creating. The paths are not to be found, but made."
4. Vision is also about *imagination*. In all cultures, over all recorded human time, people have described the power of holding a clear mental picture of the future. Athletes practice through imagery. So do physicians, musicians, architects, and engineers. We know that what we hold firmly in our mind, we can recreate in our lives. Visions are our image or expression of our hopes.

Vision Is Personal

At the group or organizational level, vision is not something you just put together in the board room along with the strategic plan, and then hand out to each employee. It can't be dictated. Nor can it simply be carried by a charismatic leader, no matter how well-intentioned it may be. In *Leadership Crisis*, Robert Greenleaf writes, "Optimal performance rests on the existence of a powerful shared vision that evolves through wide participation to which the key leader contributes, but which the use of authority cannot shape."

Vision must be born within the leader, within each member of the organization, and finally within the organization as a whole. By its very nature, vision is personal. Without this, a vision lacks energy and fails to foster commitment. For the leader who tries to simply hand a vision to his or her people, the most that can be hoped for is compliance.

What have others done to put their personal visions into words? We surfed the Web and found hundreds of personal examples, such as:

- My vision is that of a life lived with happiness, fulfillment, and value. A life centered on principles of human dignity, trust, growth, and health.
- To leave behind more than I received. To play by the rules. Take turns. Share. Listen much and talk less. To live gratefully.
- To live life completely, honestly, and compassionately.
- My vision is to have lived and played with integrity and in harmony with the universe.
- To live out loud with a sense of joy, justice, and care for the world around me.

These statements are deceptively simple. Many vision statements go on to describe in more detail what this initial statement means, how the vision will be fulfilled, and what values are implied within the vision. Complete Activity 3-1 to create a personal vision.

Vision Must Also Be Shared

If you are a charismatic leader, your own vision for the organization may be enough to carry the organization—at least for a time, and in a rather limited way. Most of the literature we've studied on the subject, in fact, points to the "need" for a leader to create the vision, then to find effective ways to communicate it to others and generate enthusiasm toward that future.

But what happens if the leader is suddenly not there?

If it's simply charisma carrying the vision, it's likely to die a quick and silent death.

Vision is not only a personal, but also a shared, ideal. A shared vision has the power to fuel enthusiasm, foster commitment, and compel people to accomplish great things—together.

Activity 3-1. What Is Your Personal Vision?

Create a vision statement for yourself, directed either toward your life as a whole or more specific to your work role. Remember that a vision does not give step-by-step instructions on how you'll achieve your goals. Your vision is a "big picture" statement of how you see yourself in the future. It's what "success" looks like. If you have trouble, imagine this scenario: You are at your retirement party and people are taking turns talking about your life. What are they saying?

My vision is to:

____

____

____

____

____

To fulfill this vision, I will:

1. ______________________________
2. ______________________________
3. ______________________________
4. ______________________________
5. ______________________________

The values I hold that are most important to me are:

1. ______________________________
2. ______________________________
3. ______________________________
4. ______________________________
5. ______________________________

This is perhaps the one most consistent hallmark of great organizations—their goals, values, missions, and visions are deeply shared. Through their vision, people are inspired to learn, to excel, and to pursue ever larger dreams simply because they want to.

You don't get a shared vision by doing the resort thing, then communicating your vision to your employees and asking for their buy-in. It becomes shared when people are directly invited and involved—in the creation of the ideal, in identifying what sets your organization apart from others, and in imagining the future. Think again about King's "I Have a Dream" speech. He was a single man, yes, but the dream he envisioned was shaped by many people, and he invited others to join together on a shared quest to bring the dream to reality.

There are many ways you can do this, whether you lead a small project team, a department, or a large organization. Here are two processes we've used to move from personal vision to a vision that's shared.

From Personal to Organizational Vision

First, invite people to create a personal vision statement, similar to the exercise you just completed. (Notice that we said "invite." Remember, vision cannot be mandated.) Encourage people to think "possibility." Offer examples of what others have done, or have people go through a values clarification exercise. If yours is a large organization, this can be done within individual departments, or in a large group setting around small tables.

Second, share these personal visions, first within smaller groups then within the large group. If needed, use facilitators to help identify what the visions have in common. Put key words and phrases up where everyone can see them.

Finally, after people have studied the key words and phrases, create a collective vision with a focus on the organization (or work group). Again, having someone to facilitate this process can be helpful.

It can also work to have someone collect each of the groups' visions and create a draft vision statement. This draft is then brought back to the groups and revised until members can agree on and share it with enthusiasm.

Future Search Processes

Using a future search conference for large-group visioning can also be effective. First, bring people together as a large group. This can involve everyone within the organization, or be a fully representative collection of stakeholders (in which case, you will want to include customers and vendors, as well). Working in small groups, have groups respond to the three questions presented at the beginning of this chapter (What is the future we desire? What do we believe in? Why do we exist—why is it important for our organization to thrive?).

Once groups have written responses to the questions, have each table report to the large group. An experienced future search facilitator will help prevent the process from getting bogged down and clarify meanings. Have recorders write down the responses. See Figure 3-1 for other questions to consider.

Figure 3-1. Questions to Invite Vision

What are we called to do?
What needs in our community or in the world are we moved to meet?
Who are we?
What are our gifts?
What do we have to contribute that's unique?
What do we value?
What do we believe in?
What do we do when we're really up against it?
What activities have "heart" for us?
What do we love doing?
What does our environment need from us?
How can we break through to our next level?

(Adapted from J. Hawley, *Reawakening the Spirit in Work*)

Yes, it can be a bit daunting to create a vision while involving large numbers of people. And we've heard many who say that it can't be done in a large group; and that it is the leader's responsibility to set the vision. During tough times, though, engaging your people is an absolute necessity. You might be surprised at just how well these processes can work, and how much energy is renewed or infused within your organization.

When writing your vision, keep in mind that the vision must be shared, attractive, valuable, credible, and easily understood. Don't waste time and energy trying to create a statement that simply sounds impressive.

Focus on What Matters

As you work to create your shared vision, keep the focus on what matters. Remember the old saying, "You will never be greater than the vision that guides you."

What does really matter in your organization? What do you value? That's what vision is about—your values. *Built to Last* author Jim Collins describes in a recent interview, "It's not what we should value—it's what we *do* value, down to our toes." He goes on to affirm what many others have also described: "Any business that exists only to make money is not enough."

What? Isn't business about making money?

Well, yes and no. Certainly an organization needs to have a financial input in order to keep things going. Unfortunately many organizations and leaders stop right there in their thinking. For them, the purpose of work lies strictly with the profit potentials.

But what if you were to take that one step further? Why is it important for the organization to survive? Answer that, and then ask again, Why is this important? Then take that answer and go one more round. And why is that important?

Complete Activity 3-2 to get to what matters.

Activity 3-2. What Matters?

What is our purpose? Why is it important for our organization to prosper?

____

____

____

And why is that important?

____

____

____

And that is important because...

____

____

____

Living Your Values

We mentioned earlier about the tendency to simply give lip service to our vision statements. We are surrounded by people who know the right words to say, but whose actions make those words meaningless. At work, this is more damaging than if the vision and values were never expressed at all. Trust is eroded. People become hard and cynical. The workplace becomes toxic and performance drops.

Leading during tough times demands integrity on your part. Your actions are consistent with your words. Your decisions are consistent with the vision that has been laid out. If you cannot support the vision through your actions, and if you don't consistently weigh decisions against that vision, then your work has been wasted.

Your values must be lived. Keep your vision in front at all times. When making a decision on a new product, reorganizing a work unit, even remodeling, remember to ask, "Is this what we do? Is this consistent with our vision?"

Begin with the End in Sight

We cannot predict the future. But we often overlook the fact that we can, and should, imagine it. That's what this "vision thing" is all about.

Once you have a clear vision in front of you, you can begin working backward from that desired future. The question, really, is quite simple: *What needs to happen in order to make this vision a reality?*

On your own or with others, try Activity 3-3.

Activity 3-3. Imagining the Future

Awards

A. Imagine yourself five years from now. You are at an awards banquet honoring your organization as *Absolute #1 Greatest Company in America!* Describe at least seven characteristics of your workplace that have resulted in your getting this most prestigious award.

1. ____________________
2. ____________________
3. ____________________
4. ____________________
5. ____________________
6. ____________________
7. ____________________

B. Now, think about your organization today. Given its present course (be honest here!), create at least one "reality" award. Here are some "award starters":

Most ____________________

Best ____________________

For outstanding achievement in

____

C. Finally, look at your responses above. What will it take to shift from B to A? Write down the three most important steps you can take to achieve A.

1. ____________________
2. ____________________
3. ____________________

Activity 3-3 (continued)

Annual Report for 2010

The key to creating a new future, even during the toughest times, is to envision that future then look back to the present to find your way. With your work unit, imagine what your annual report for 2010 will look like—what you wish it to be. Now, create that report. It can become the foundation and inspiration for doing extraordinary work today!

Chapter Four: Mindfulness

"In the beginner's mind there are many possibilities,
but in the expert's there are few."
(Shunryu Suzuki)

There is a great tendency in our society to act from mindlessness. Terri likes to refer to this as "the Duh Factor." As in, a red light means you stop. You didn't stop. You created an accident. Maybe you should have stopped. Well, Duh. Or, how do you reduce turnover? You create the kind of workplace that people want to be a part of. Duh.

Mindlessness is the condition of acting without fully using our minds—acting without a critical awareness, thoughtfulness, or full attention. Think of some of the things people do in a mindless way: eating in front of the television when bored; running our fingers through our hair when feeling tense; performing a routine task like washing the dishes or mowing the yard; placing that square widget in the square hole; assigning parking places; creating hierarchies and bureaucracies because "that's how things get done."

Mindlessness happens for several reasons. It happens because of habits we develop. It happens because we don't think about what we're doing or about the consequences of our actions. It happens because of the mental images we hold of how the world should be. And it happens because of distinctions we have formed, such as what is old or young, ugly or beautiful, success or failure, good or bad. We avoid critical thinking.

Using a mindless approach to tasks and decisions can make things quick and easy. We don't have to think about anything. But it also limits us. We find ourselves doing things just because it's how we've always done them, or thinking a certain way because we've always thought that way. We preserve the status quo.

Mindless leadership has resulted in organizations built like the *Titanic*—solid and stable in appearance, but difficult to maneuver when change is critical. We've put together complex communication channels for a smooth, deliberate flow of information, only to be frustrated by sluggishness and twisted messages. We've set zero-tolerance policies, and then been shocked when all sense of wisdom in justice seems to have been erased. We've outlined processes and procedures, built organizational charts and structures to enhance efficiency, only to be puzzled by the learned helplessness and lack of critical thinking that set in.

We forget that things are as we have made them, intentionally or not. At any time we can choose to take a more mindful approach and stop being victims to our mindlessness.

In tough times, the Duh Factor has to be eliminated—totally—or times will get even tougher. The ability and willingness to challenge the status quo and approach our work and our role mindfully are hallmarks of the most vital organizations.

Leading Mindfully

Leading mindfully involves paying careful attention to what's around us—the full context in which we work. It's openness to looking at our workplace in new ways. We like the idea of the Japanese Shoshin, or beginner's mind. This is the ability to keep one's mind open, to be outwardly focused, and to see everything as if for the first time. Rather than limiting ourselves by saying things like "I know what this is" or "I have attained this," we always choose to be a beginner.

With the mindfulness that comes with a beginner's mind, we are better able to seek opportunities that go beyond "how we do things." Out-of-the-box thinking is about mindfulness. So is the ability to erase traditional boundaries. Living and working mindfully calls for the ability and willingness to think critically, to question everything around us, and to challenge traditional norms and authorities.

When Ricardo Semler, president of the Brazilian multinational company Semco, decided his health could no longer survive leading his company in a traditional way, he took a mindful approach to change. As he examined his company's current structure, he realized he had been leading the company in a mindless way. He had simply been following what his father had done before him and what he saw other managers and leaders doing. So he turned the job of managing work over to the people at work.

Employees hired and fired managers. They selected members of their own work teams, created smaller facilities so that people would know who they worked with, and developed business literacy through open book management. As they developed, the people of Semco initiated their own product development; determined locations for new sites; made decisions concerning profit sharing; and even began setting their own salaries. They rethought their relationship with their union and found new ways to work together.

Ricardo Semler's ability to critically examine company habits and to question why they did things the way they did has had great impact. He turned a business teetering on collapse into a company of people who have thrived even in the toughest economic times. Oh yes, Semco's profits grew 900 percent in 12 years. Semco is one of the world's most profitable companies.

How do you lead with mindfulness? Here are five basic approaches to doing your work and being a leader that help you see work with a beginner's mind.

Challenge the Status Quo

The first action is to challenge the status quo. Tough times demand some kind of organizational change. If there was no need for change, it wouldn't be a tough time. But it is impossible to embrace change while preserving the status quo. The two simply do not go together. When we're trapped in old habits and mindsets, we don't see our potential. We get stuck in our problems and turn to blaming others: "That was a terrible decision." "We should never have left that market." "Who hired that bozo anyway?" Conflict becomes damaging rather than energizing. People burn out. The environment becomes toxic. Change is elusive, and development impossible.

Leading mindfully requires a way of viewing the world—and the workplace—as something new and fresh, every day. It requires attention to new information and a commitment to viewing problems as opportunities.

Sure, we hear that all the time. And it's usually easier said than done.

Yet it is critical that the organization is willing and able to reflect on itself and to critique and question relationships, structures, and "how we do things." It is only through raising questions, considering what could be rather than what is, that we can thrive even during the most difficult of times.

That willingness and ability begins with you, the leader. It also begins while times are good, which we'll discuss more in a later chapter.

Turn Off Your Automatic Pilot

The second mindfulness action is to turn off your autopilot. People engage in a great deal of complicated behavior without paying much attention to what they are doing—mindlessly. Think of how often you drive someplace, only to get there and realize you don't remember a thing about the trip. There are few things as complicated, both physically and cognitively, as carefully steering thousands of pounds of steel down a busy roadway. We have to pay attention to our speed, braking, where other vehicles are in relation to us, weather conditions, pedestrians, and bicyclists.

We check for hazards in the road and maneuver around them. We check mileage and read road signs. We sing with the radio. We eat, put on makeup, talk on the cell phone, even read e-mail. We break up the kids' argument in the back seat and mentally replay a conversation from work. In order to do all these things, and more, we put some of our actions on automatic pilot.

This happens many times throughout our day: We type without reading what we are typing from, jog without remembering what we saw, feed the kids while reading the mail and talking on the phone. We value "multitasking." We perform acts without any mindful attention to what we're doing, based on our previous habits and experience. We set ourselves on automatic pilot.

Acting on automatic pilot during a critical time in your organization, however, will be disastrous, just as it can be when you're driving and someone in a car next to you unexpectedly moves into your lane, or a child suddenly runs out into the street. If we're lucky, our reactions are quick enough to avoid a tragic ending. In our organizations, however, we can't rely on this kind of luck.

During the 1980s and 1990s, for example, companies laid off millions of people in order to quickly reduce costs. It became so common that it was almost habitual. If costs needed to be cut, the easiest way was to eliminate jobs. Yet research has consistently shown over 20 years that downsizing is among the *least effective* ways to achieve financial goals. It should be a last, rather than first, resort. For many decision-makers today, though, laying off people has become a form of automatic behavior. Costs are high, profits are down, and people are expendable. So they cut—deeply and swiftly—only to regret it later when they struggle to meet minimal performance goals, scramble to recover from bad press, and wonder how they can possibly rebuild their status as being a good place to work.

Automatic behavior results in self-imposed constraints and inflexible thinking, making it impossible to meet new challenges. We over-rely on standard operating procedures—our organizational habits. To illustrate this, try an experiment used by many creativity leaders. During one of your work unit meetings, draw this figure and ask people to imagine that it is a cake.

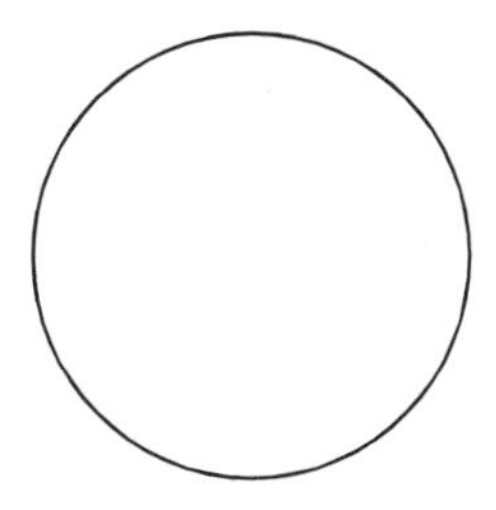

Ask people to slice the cake into as many pieces as possible, using only four straight cuts. How many pieces of cake can they come up with? Many people will come up with 8 pieces—a standard cake-cut. Your more efficient one-dimensional thinkers will come up with 11 pieces of cake.

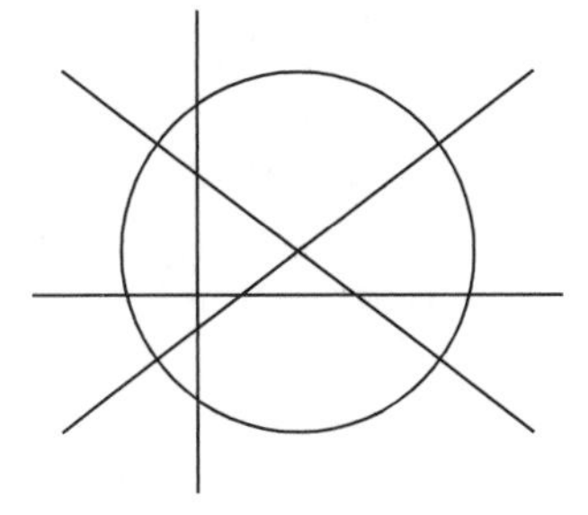

Remember, though, that cakes are three-dimensional. If you make the first three cuts vertical, you'll have seven pieces. If you make your fourth cut horizontal, you now have 14 pieces.

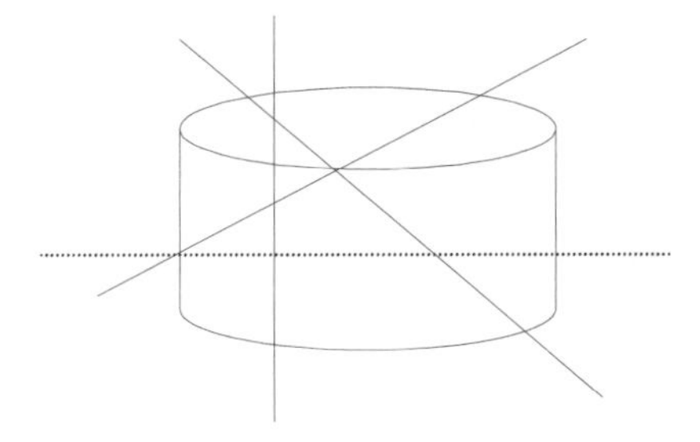

For a long time, Brian Biro, the creator of this game, believed 14 was the perfect answer—end of exercise—until he had a workshop participant show him his own inflexible thinking. Using four perfectly straight lines, this woman approached the problem in a new way, coming up with 16 pieces by adding a new dimension.

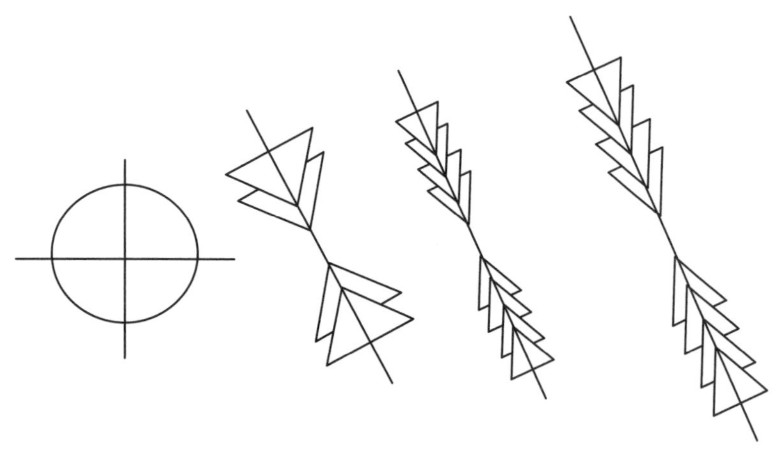

With your work unit, talk about what everyone was thinking when confronted with the cake-cutting problem. Then take it a step further: What habits are your group using mindlessly? How might things be improved by taking a different perspective, or by looking at the cake differently? When we're leading during tough times, the ability to thrive depends on our ability to identify and break free of limiting habits, mindsets, and SOPs. To lead in tough times, you must create a safe environment to help make mindfulness the norm, rather than the exception.

When your organization is going through a difficult time, make sure your automatic pilot has been firmly turned to "Off." Taking action strictly out of habit will be self-defeating. Though quick decisions will no doubt be needed, make sure you pause long enough to ask yourself:

- Am I doing this because I have carefully thought it through, considered the possible outcomes, and weighed the options?
- Or, am I doing this because this is what I have always done, or what I see others doing?

Actively seek input from a diverse group of people. Encourage your people to challenge your decisions. Challenge the status quo. Engage others in helping you spot whatever might be wrong with the action. Refuse to take mindless action.

Act from Multiple Perspectives

The third action of mindfulness is to act from multiple, not single, perspectives. People often act as if there were one, and only one, set of rules for any number of circumstances—only one perspective from which to act. Many of us grew up believing that there was a certain way one's home should look. There was a hard-and-fast rule for keeping house: always neat and tidy, dusted, vacuumed, a place for everything and everything in its place. Thousands of women have driven themselves nearly to the point of lunacy trying to earn a paycheck, raise a family, and keep house the way it was "supposed" to be—the way the rule said.

Just as we sometimes think the house should look a certain way, we create similar rules for table manners, or how people should dress, or what a cluttered desk at work says about a person, or how things should happen at work, or whether it's appropriate for the new clerk to talk casually with the CEO. We often judge others and take action from a very limited, single perspective. What happens? We close our minds to alternative ways of thinking and of solving problems. We can walk right by the answer we need that's been in front of us all the time. Duh.

Maybe there is value in being able to write "I Love You" in the furniture dust.

In similar mindless ways, we might rely on the "experts" to tell us what to do or think—a favorite news correspondent, political figure, or management guru. Our limited perspectives are comfortable, like an old pair of shoes we can easily slip into. Single perspectives, however, lead us into a kind of mental laziness, accepting things at face value without thinking critically about them. This kind of mindset adds to our tendency to over-generalize and act from some preconceived set of rules, and to typecast and view others through our own biases. We search for evidence that confirms our beliefs, rather than challenging those beliefs by considering multiple perspectives.

The leaders of a company we worked with spoke often of the need for continuous improvement within their work processes. Yet, when two key departments were at odds over how customer orders were handled, the leaders attacked the problem from a single perspective. Rather than looking for answers from multiple perspectives, they turned to what they knew best. They looked at how their industry traditionally handled this common disconnect.

The department that spoke directly with customers promised complex services and scheduled the technical service providers. The technical department responsible for filling these orders was frustrated because the services were unreasonable given the promised timeframe for completion. So what did the leaders do? They coached the two department heads to improve communication and had employees take part in separate (yes, separate) teambuilding activities. The result, not surprising, was that nothing really changed. Duh.

In contrast, another company was experiencing similar tensions between functional departments. Instead of relying on their existing perspective, however, the leaders challenged everyone involved to push beyond the problem, investigate creative options, and test their top choices. Employees created a cross-functional task force to explore options, and everyone was involved in selecting their top choices. It's true nothing changed for a while—and yet, in many ways, everything changed. Structures remained the same, but now people were engaged in finding a solution. They were energized.

Employees of all levels were actively looking for alternative perspectives on how they could best serve their customers and each other. Ultimately they created an integrated system that reduced turnaround time, thrilled customers, and strengthened the relationships between people with different skills and work roles. Though unplanned, this process also increased people's sense of commitment to the company. And, as you would imagine, it triggered a series of similar mindful examinations of other work procedures.

Was it quick and easy? Nope. It wasn't painless, either. And some people criticized the CEO for not simply telling them what to do. But it worked—tremendously.

It will take courage for you, as a leader, to lead mindfully and consider multiple perspectives. Challenging the status quo is rarely a popular action. It disrupts our comfort zones when we're pushed for sound judgment and a more reflective approach to work. Leading in tough times takes a certain boldness, a certain audacity. You must be willing to question how things are done. You must also be capable of sometimes brutal self-criticism and circumspection in order to challenge your own mindset and seek new perspectives.

Believe in Unlimited Resources

The fourth action for mindful leadership is to throw away the concept of limited resources. We get stuck in that zero sum game—if we give more here, we have less over there. The result is that we set rigid limits that narrow our sights, our choices, and our imagination. Mindlessness has a chance to grow. During the tough times at work, the tendency is even greater than usual to view our workplaces as having limited resources. Usually this involves money as the main issue.

Most of us have grown up being taught that there are limits to things. I can't count the number of times as a child I heard some version of "money doesn't grow on trees, you know." What resources do you see as being limited? Take a piece of paper and divide it into two columns. Head one column Personal Life, the other Organization. Now write down all the resources you see as being limited in Activity 4-1.

Activity 4-1. Limited Resources

In my personal life...	**In my organization...**

What did you list? Terri listed money, natural resources, energy, abilities, and time. Now consider this: Are these resources really limited, or are we placing limits on them?

At work, it's easy to see our resources as limited when we're forced by market changes to cut costs and do more with less. We hold on to and protect what we have. The danger in this kind of thinking is that our efforts to conserve can also hold us back. We restrict our sense of purpose, creativity, even our world view. We set false limits because we are afraid we will run out of something. The result is, of course, that we rarely make full use of what is available to us. In our effort to protect what we have, we don't consider what else is possible.

What if, instead of analyzing limited resources, we shifted our mindset and proceeded as though our resources could be improved upon? What we seek with money, for example, is really simply a state of mind, once certain basic human needs are met. What we often seek with our dollars are things that are already in abundance (and don't cost a thing)—excitement, confidence, respectability, love. We argue and struggle with ways to put our minds and talents to preserving natural resources, when greater energy could be put into exploring the limitless other ways to fulfill those functions. We push energies and abilities to what we believe are our limits, and stop—rarely testing to see whether these are true limits or not.

During a significant growth spurt in his company, Relationship Marketing, Inc., president Jim Lewis was faced with all kinds of new problems. Space was a big one. There just didn't seem to be enough space for everyone to work effectively. As new people came in and others were promoted, associates challenged why Joe got an office, but Sally didn't. Work areas were always being shifted, expanded, condensed. People's tempers were getting short and the innovation vital for their success was at risk.

Jim's leader team understood that the physical environment was posing new challenges for them, but relocating was not a good option. For a time, Jim and his team puzzled over how to get everyone to fit well within the space they had: "What if Dave is here and Judith over there? No, Creative has to be here and Shipping goes there." They were getting nowhere. Then, they shifted their focus.

What if, instead of trying to make the people fit the environment, they changed the environment to fit what people really needed? So they took time to find out just what people did need. The result was a highly innovative and energizing reconstruction of their facility. Ample private and community areas were designed. Rich textures, lighting, colors, even playthings were used to soothe and to stimulate. An arena was created for large gatherings, with seating designed to encourage interaction rather than one-way communication. People were involved in defining just what they needed to be most effective, and the company worked to make sure people had it.

One very major problem was where to put a growing call center. Solution: use the cake-cutting approach. They viewed their existing space multidimensionally, and created a new floor where none had existed. Result: expanded workspace without adding to their real estate.

Jim Lewis and the people at Relationship Marketing had been stuck by their focus on analyzing their limited resources (space). Once they were able to shift their mindset and see their resources as being improvable and unlimited, they were able to create workspace in which everyone could thrive.

Think of all the things during the 20th century that people said couldn't be done because we'd reached the limits already. And yet people proved they could be done: breaking the five-minute mile, then the four-minute mile; landing on the moon; glasses so small they fit on your eyes (contact lenses); auto mileage exceeding 20 mpg; a global communication network that puts people in contact with the whole world at the touch of a button.

In each case, false limits had been set, then challenged by a few courageous people. Leading mindfully means constantly reassessing your resources, double-checking that you are not setting false limits, and trying out ways to improve upon your resources.

Go back to the resources lists you made a little while ago. Examine each item you listed.

- Which resources are you not testing the limits to?
- Where have you imposed false limits?
- What would happen if you changed your perception?
- What are ways you can improve upon the resources you have available?
- How can you use your resources differently?

Turn your paper over and start writing out your ideas. Sit down with your work unit and do a similar activity. Challenge people to shift their mindsets and think about and act from possibility rather than limits.

Encourage Mindfulness in Others

The fifth action is to actively encourage mindfulness in others. It's not enough to lead mindfully if everyone else around you insists on the status quo. Part of your responsibility as a leader is to increase capacity—increase people's ability to thoughtfully approach problems, act with courage, and respond appropriately to changes in the environment.

In many organizations, people have worked hard to make certain actions automatic—to reduce the need for a more mindful approach to work. While this can help speed processes or standardize some results, it also reduces a person's need to think about what they are doing, to consider better ways, and to push for an improvement.

How else can you as a leader encourage mindfulness? Here are several actions:

1. Model a questioning approach to how work is organized and conducted; make it everyone's responsibility to question, critique, and challenge decisions.
2. Eliminate routine as much as possible. Put job enrichment strategies in place. Examine work processes to find and eliminate areas where people are able to work mindlessly.
3. Encourage people to look at their work in new ways. Make "Why?" and "What if...?" part of everyone's day.
4. Share jobs. Cross-train. Give people every opportunity to view their work from multiple perspectives.
5. Regularly challenge "the way things are done around here." Engage people in questioning their assumptions, ideas, principles, and attitudes.
6. Get different people working together to encourage new combinations and ideas.
7. Meet in new and novel places to stimulate new ideas. Value novelty and playfulness. They are the triggers for creativity.
8. When conflicts come up, don't be too quick to compromise. Innovations come from the willingness to hold the tensions.
9. Increase people's business literacy by having employees regularly review the numbers for your business or department—profits, project outcomes, costs, etc. Find ways to publicly display your work unit's progress and successes.
10. Create a safe environment for taking risks. Nothing new comes from doing things the same way.
11. Eliminate fear. Be accepting that mistakes will happen, and involve everyone in learning from them.
12. Increase peoples' control of their own work. Don't be so quick to jump in to solve problems for others.

13. Find ways to gain new information from diverse sources. Have people regularly explore other departments, other businesses, other ways of doing things.
14. Set goals that are challenging but realistic.
15. Expect great things from your people.

You eliminate the mindlessness (and the Duh Factor) by using a beginner's mind and working with mindfulness. As you lead in tough times, ask yourself the following questions:

____ Do I challenge the status quo?

____ Have I turned off my automatic pilot?

____ Do I look for solutions from multiple perspectives?

____ Do I look at resources as unlimited, limited only by my lack of imagination?

____ Do I continually encourage mindfulness?

Chapter Five: Engaging Others

"If you want [people] to act like it's their business,
make it their business."
(Belasco & Stayer, ***Flight of the Buffalo***)

Scott Simmerman, the creator of Square Wheels® development tools and programs, likes to say, "No one ever washes a rental car." There's a great deal of truth in that simple statement. When people lack ownership, they often lack full commitment as well. With commitment comes careful attention to what is being done. We need that, especially during the tough times.

Lots of companies have moved to participatory management, and much has been written about participation and involvement. For many companies, that's enough. But during the tough times, you want full engagement and ownership.

To engage someone means more than simply asking them to give input on a decision or to participate on a team. Think of how gears work, how they are engaged: the separate parts come together and interlock in a way that significantly boosts an operation's strength and performance.

When people are engaged, they voluntarily commit their minds, hearts, and talents. Involvement is when people come together around a work issue.

Engagement is the sense of ownership or commitment it takes to trigger innovation, nurture community, and get the job done in the best way possible. People interlock with other people, and tremendous things happen. Engaged people are involved, yes; but all involved people are not necessarily engaged.

During the tough times, make sure people aren't renting the car, they're owning it.

The Need for Involvement

Research on organizational change and development is very consistent: If you want to create a meaningful, sustainable change and a high performance workplace, involve people directly in making the decisions and implementing the actions that affect their work. It's a no-brainer (Duh). And yet it's surprising how seldom this happens in a real way.

A while ago we were talking with a production manager at a manufacturing plant about the company's attempts to implement high involvement work practices after 18 years with a more traditional management structure. The manager described, "It's just not working. We tell people that we want their input, put them into work teams, and yet nothing happens. Maybe it works in other places, but these people just won't do it. They don't get it."

More likely, his workplace has created some learned helplessness. The classic Taylorist approach to work still dominates today's workplace, in spite of the push for greater participation. One of the most harmful unintended consequences of these workplaces is the occurrence of learned helplessness. And it was taught by the very work processes, procedures, and detailed handbooks that were intended to boost performance. When one person controls someone else's work, learned helplessness can set in.

What does that mean? We quite literally learn to be helpless. Like a Dilbert comic strip, people learn to turn off their brains when they walk through the company door and operate mindlessly until the end of their shift. More times than not, people's behavior is a symptom, and not the problem itself. The system has been the problem, if not in your organization then some other classically run institution in which the person has been involved.

It happens when people aren't asked to think, or when choice and control over people's work life are taken from them. People are told what to do and how to do it. All around us we still have companies where people have to ask permission to use the restroom, and bells tell them when to change tasks or take a break. When we don't have to think, we learn to stop thinking. When our ideas are shot down often enough, we learn to stop having ideas—or at least to stop opening our mouth.

The creativity, critical-thinking, and problem-solving skills that are used in other areas of our life can seem nonexistent at work. Futility sets in and people become passive even in situations where they do have control and voice. We see this repeatedly in organizations trying to shift from a more traditional management style to a flatter, more participatory environment. As the manufacturing manager described, it appears that people just "don't get it."

There isn't an organization around today that can afford to allow learned helplessness to grow, or to be present at all. And we cannot afford operating from single views and perspectives that come with a more traditional way of conducting work.

We need the creativity, the drive, and the thoughtfulness that occur when people come together to work toward a common goal, when they are actively involved in creating their own work life, and when they are engaged mindfully. We need the multiple perspectives. The more people we can engage in participative behavior, the more we can access its potentials and the wiser we can become. And we reduce the occurrence of learned helplessness.

Our organizations become more intelligent and responsive through involvement and participation, through the sharing of problems and ideas, and even through conflict.

Remember, though, that it took time to teach helplessness. And it might take time for people to learn another way to be at work. If you are asking your people to participate, and they seem reluctant or unable, be persistent. And look for ways to further engage them.

Involvement and Participation Today

Sure, everyone talks about involvement and participation today. The Employment Policy Foundation research shows a self-reported 68 percent adoption rate among large employers, and some studies show this rate to be 90 percent and higher. It's hard to pick up a current management book without something in it about involvement. But when push comes to shove, when times get really tough, the greater tendency is for leaders to take back the reins—to take back control.

During the tough times, this won't help you. Whether it's a downsizing or a slump in the stock market, you need greater flexibility, new perspectives, and the commitment of every member of your workforce. You don't get that through control or through token involvement, no matter how well-intentioned. You get it by making sure people are fully engaged in their work.

The Appearance of Involvement

In too many organizations, involvement is more a matter of appearance than of a real and meaningful change in how work is conducted, or in the division of power, authority, and profit. And employees know that.

We call it involvement when we ask for people's input, push decision-making to the front-line people, set up teams, create quality circles, or implement gain-sharing and profit-sharing programs. And that's good. But far too often, input is ignored. Decision-making is supported only when the CEO gives his or her blessing. Quality circles get mired in bureaucratic detail. Except in rare cases, the use of teams and the division of power and profits are determined by those who hold the power. Participation is shallow, at best, when the really "important" decisions continue to be made in the traditional ways.

Yes it's true that we are involving more people in today's workplace—to a greater or lesser degree—but are we really engaging them?

From Involvement to Engagement

Twenty years ago, Ford began a journey to transform an autocratic work environment into a self-empowered culture based on trust, respect, and collaboration. At about the same time, Ricardo Semler made a similar decision with his company, Semco, and stood their top-down structure on its head. AES, Harley Davidson, SAS, and many other well-known and lesser-known organizations organized themselves in similar ways and have seen tremendous gains as a result. At the heart of these "new" work environments lies a focus on engaging the whole person in how work is organized and conducted.

Involvement brings people together around a common work issue. Engagement instills ownership. It's the meshing of the gears. It goes beyond job satisfaction to a state of authentic participation, contribution, and ownership.

When leading in tough times, you want to make some changes happen, and great things are possible when we increase participation: a greater sense of ownership, more diverse skills, increased wisdom and knowledge, increased creativity and innovation, a heightened sense of community, and the sharing of wisdom. On the more "practical" side, companies using participatory practices attribute 70 percent of their productivity growth to employee involvement and realize productivity gains averaging 18 percent to 25 percent. Productivity gains can jump 200 percent and higher for companies that have adopted even more self-organizing, self-directing practices.

It takes, though, a willingness to share the power, share the authority, even share the profits, and to give up trying to control everything.

Basics of Engagement

Many organizations today engage their employees. Here are a few examples:

- At Semco, employees hire their managers, divide profits, create their own work groups, and decide where their CEO's office should be. Some set their own salaries or take several months to identify where within the company they can be of most use.

- At Cascades, transparency is critical, and people are free to talk to the press or the public about their workplace at any time. There is no official spokesperson. Work is conducted in a way that won't shame anyone.
- At SAS, everyone has their own office. Everyone.
- At Weitz Construction, democratic work processes are in place.
- At Relationship Marketing, Inc., play is as important as work.
- At Bertch Cabinet Manufacturing, the company includes a campus of several buildings; each building is limited to about 200 employees so that people have a greater sense of community with the people with whom they work. No one is lost in a crowd of thousands.
- At Great Harvest Bread, you can be fired for regularly working more than 40 hours a week. Work should be in the interest of your life; your life shouldn't be in the interest of work.

All around are organizations that have taken "involvement" one step further and work to fully engage people in what they do. Some are union, some are not. Some are large, some are small. Some are local, some are global. They are in vastly different industries—for-profits and non-profits, structured and unstructured. But they all have something in common: a deep interest in engaging the whole person and in making involvement a real, rather than appropriated, experience. They pursue ownership and full engagement.

By now you may be wondering, "OK, so just how do I do that? What steps do I take?" Sorry, but we can't give you a formula for that. There isn't one. It looks different in each organization. The path each organization has taken is unique. The structures and processes are different.

You and your employees are the only ones who can determine what this will look like for your organization. Engagement starts with full participation right from the beginning. You can't take an autocratic approach to high involvement (though many people try). You can't call an employee meeting and announce that you want everyone to be more engaged in what they do. People will likely just sit back and wait for you to tell them what it is you want to happen.

But as we study different organizations that promote engagement, we do see some common actions and beliefs of leaders. These include the following:

- *Support local control and capacity-building.* Put choices, power, and authority as close to the work as possible. Encourage everyone to challenge their assumptions about what is possible.
- *Share the profits.* And let the people determine the division. By placing profit sharing in the hands of each unit, people will also increase their understanding of the economics of the business and develop their financial literacy. Ownership will become real.
- *Persist.* When things don't seem to work out, hold firmly to your beliefs. Take a new approach. Involve people in working through the kinks. Commit to an engaged workforce.
- *Care for the whole.* As a leader, you are responsible for more than a successful business. You are also accountable for the well-being of the community in which your organization operates. Be an active participant, and find ways to encourage your workforce to actively care as well.
- *Be vulnerable.* No one expects you to be right all the time or to always work perfectly. When something doesn't work, take the blame and leave it. Acknowledge the failures, disappointments, and shortfalls, then move on confidently.
- *Speak in simple, direct language.* Stay simple and direct: no flowery speeches, no rationalizations, no forced optimism.
- *Value the human system first.* You work with people—people, living and breathing, like you, who share with you the same concerns, desires, dreams, joys, and defeats. They are neither pieces of equipment nor part of your assets. The technical elements of work will always be secondary to the human element. Cultivate a safe environment in which people can fully interact.
- *Name what matters.* And keep it in front of you. In all that you do, ask: Are my actions consistent with what I have said matters to me and matters within our organization?

Creating an Ownership Environment

People support what they create. They care for what they own.

People perform best when they can influence their work and control their environment; when they are engaged; when they can act as owners, rather than reacting to the desires of others; when they work with collaborative goals.

A sense of ownership helps create a personal connection to the organization and inspires people to contribute. It strengthens people and builds your internal capacity as people increase their knowledge of the business, assess their own outcomes, and learn by seeing directly what works and what doesn't.

Though how this happens looks different in each organization, there are similar actions that different leaders and work groups have taken to achieve an ownership mindset.

1. Make Involvement Voluntary Rather Than Mandatory

Mandates are made based on one person's power over another. This is what you are trying to eliminate. We can't force people to "take ownership" of their work. Attempting to do so would defeat our purpose right from the start. But we can create conditions at work that engage people in ways that make ownership both attractive and possible. People become willing to invest themselves—to invest in the company, invest in their jobs, and invest emotionally in their work. Participation may begin slowly, with a few brave souls jumping in. But as more jump, and as others see the results, participation and engagement will become the norm rather than the exception. As the leader, it is up to you to provide the resources and opportunity to let this happen, and to do whatever you can to enhance individual and collective development.

2. Invite Full Participation and Strengthen Others

Have those responsible for implementing something make the decision and develop the plan for themselves. It doesn't matter how brilliant a plan is; it just doesn't work to ask people to sign on when they haven't been involved in creating it. People need to be able to personally interact with a plan—be co-creators of it. Make use of focus groups, project teams, and task forces. Draw on your internal expertise. When expertise is lacking, encourage people to find it.

This doesn't leave you out; you too are part of this work community. But you can ask questions more than you direct. You can speak last. You can solicit opinions and ideas rather than always offering your own. You can ask people to make decisions, take action, assess results, and learn from what they are doing. You can host daily huddles with your work unit and help other people become more comfortable with listening to others and telling their own ideas. Create conditions where others can be strengthened.

3. Embrace the Process

It's the participation process that is critical—that makes a plan come alive for each person. Then people can commit to it because it has become more real for them. Oftentimes this means decisions are made more slowly. Then again, you might be surprised, once people have developed a sense of ownership, just how much more quickly things can happen. No longer will rigid structures and chains of command get in the way of creative work.

The process, though, can be frustrating. There will be times when you take an idea to people, see it torn apart, thrown out, brought back, and finally approved in a form much like its initial one. It can be an amazing but necessary process. If a change involves the whole system, then involve the whole system in the decision, the planning, and the implementation. The work can be intense, but new and surprising perspectives become available.

4. Let People Accept Responsibility

This is a biggie. So often we hear, "But our people just won't accept responsibility." In most cases that we've seen, it's not so much a matter of people not accepting responsibility. It's a matter of managers and other designated leaders who won't let go of responsibility. Or they give it then take it back.

Take this quick self-assessment:

- Are there actions I sometimes take that prevent people from doing their jobs? For example, do I ask someone to troubleshoot a piece of equipment, then quickly suggest what might be wrong? Or ask someone to write a memo, only to end up telling them what I want it to say?
- Do I dominate meetings? Do I direct what is going on, set the schedule, reserve the room? Or do I share tasks with others, without criticism concerning their decisions?
- Do I intentionally or unintentionally intimidate others with my words, tone, or body language?
- Do I offer my opinions first, before listening to those of others?
- When someone poses a problem to me, am I quick to offer a solution?
- Do I often finish other people's sentences?

- Do I cut off people when they are speaking, or try to "multi-task" while I'm listening?
- Do I take on tasks myself, because someone else isn't doing it fast enough or the way I would?
- How often do I change the meeting agenda, raising issues that no one else is prepared for?

These are all subtle and not-so-subtle signs that you may be preventing others from taking responsibility. Take some time to think about what your role as leader really is. Is it to direct and control what takes place in your work area? Or is it to serve as a resource provider, to keep the vision in full view, nurture learning and development, and cultivate energy? With the former, about the best you can hope for is compliance. As a resource provider, you can engage others.

Yes, there are times when employees will wait for you to tell them exactly what to do. There are times when uncertainty sets in. There are times when no one else seems to want to speak up. There are times when employees look to you in an almost parental way, and you'll be tempted to step into that role.

Learn to wait out these tensions. By stepping in for others, you deny them the opportunity to develop themselves—to step up to the responsibility. You are working with adults. Treat them as such. And expect adult behavior and adult responsibilities from them. Remember that responsibility is a learned behavior and attitude. Every time you take this back, you reinforce the idea that you, not they, are responsible.

5. Build Trust

Ownership and full engagement won't happen without trust. Trust is what replaces the controls that will be removed. The ideal, of course, is that trust is there until someone proves untrustworthy. But that's often not the way it works.

Your organization may be one of thousands where fear and distrust have eroded relationships. Understand that rebuilding trust will take time and a concerted, persistent effort. In these situations, it is understandable that people will be reluctant to trust and quick to question your motives.

An interesting dynamic about trust—and distrust—is how very contagious it is. When you show trust of others, others are more likely to put their trust in you and in their co-workers. Likewise, if you show distrust, people are less likely to trust you and others.

Building trust is a process that begins when one person risks opening up to another. Through personal disclosure, you demonstrate your trust in people. This encourages them to trust you. Interact honestly with others. Richard Gutherie, author of *Working with Spirit: To Replace Control With Trust*, describes, "In business, truth is a very powerful change agent." Use it.

As the leader, trust others with information. Disclose information about who you are, your beliefs, your values. Use active listening techniques; listen attentively and eagerly. Seek out others for informal conversations. Push for open or transparent communication. Ask questions. Admit mistakes and say, "I don't know" when you don't know. Step in to help others. And ask others for help. Speak positively about other people.

6. Practice Conversation

Margaret Wheatley frequently talks about the need to rediscover the art of conversation and the importance of it—not mediation or negotiation; not problem-solving, debate, or public meetings; no agendas, hidden or otherwise. We're talking about simple, truthful conversation where we each have a chance to speak on an issue, we each feel heard, and we each listen well. As Wheatley describes, conversation "is the most ancient and easiest way to cultivate the conditions for change."

Sit together, and talk about what's important to us. Discuss the undiscussable. Meet for lunch. Test ideas. Find out how people feel about their work and the workplace. Do they feel engaged? Don't trust your intentions; find out if people are invested in their work.

Yes, it takes time, attention, and quite often a willingness to be uncomfortable. But the payoff far surpasses the discomforts.

7. Get Out of the Middle

Stop being in the middle of everything or you'll own the responsibilities, too. Leave your ego at the door. Don't insist people learn how to do it your way; they'll put all their time and energy in trying to learn your way, rather than in doing what they do best, what you hired them for.

You don't need to have every little detail checked with you. You don't even need to be kept constantly informed. Your people own the responsibility for their own performance, for delivering great performance, and for learning from their performance. You are responsible for creating the environment where this can take place.

Are You Creating Owners?

Within most organizations, true ownership, engagement, and collaboration simply do not exist—at least, not in real and meaningful ways. And that's not surprising. After all, this way of conducting work demands extremely high levels of trust, and the willingness to widely share power and authority. Even our formal reward systems discourage it. Most of us have been conditioned to value the "Lone Ranger" approach, where our success rests on our individual skill and initiative. Our major institutions reinforce this; our schools even tend to punish collaboration.

But the fact remains: In most cases, collective problem-solving and decision-making result in better solutions and decisions. When we engage with others—working together toward a meaningful goal that we share—and when we draw on our collective knowledge and wisdom, tremendous things happen. As the saying goes, nobody is as smart as everybody.

People who are fully engaged at work and who interlock with others approach their work differently. They view their investments differently in terms of their time, energy, emotion, and knowledge. They become more adaptive, and more effective at surviving and thriving during the tough times.

Remember:

1. Make involvement voluntary rather than mandatory
2. Invite full participation and strengthen others
3. Embrace the process
4. Let people accept responsibility
5. Build trust
6. Practice conversation
7. Get out of the middle

Chapter Six: Re-energizing Work

"Life must be lived as play."
(Plato)

In spite of our best intentions to work hard, to rally the troops, and to shine through a difficult period of time, the fact remains: tough times can drain and deaden us, robbing us of our energy, attention, passion, commitment, and concern for others.

The strain that often accompanies times of uncertainty can lead us to focus narrowly on our own survival, either as an individual, a group, or an organization. Understandable, yes, but it makes further development difficult, if not impossible. Defensive strategies will never be enough. Too often they lead to a toxic environment in which to work—an environment that poisons, deadens, and drains the spirit as people are treated as objects of production. At a time when peoples' energies and high spirits are critical, and when creativity and collaborative work are vital, you can't afford to risk this. It is this deadening of spirit that can make sound change initiatives fail, stunt innovation, and destroy the energy and momentum needed to make things work.

So what does it take to help people maintain their energy, to keep moving forward rather than back? While there's no recipe book to pluck off the shelf and put into place, we do know that organizations that thrive during tough times have several common characteristics.

Be in It Together

One of the most powerful ways to garner support for new efforts, build the courage to press forward, and energize flagging spirits is to show, in both real and symbolic ways, that you really are in this together. Years of research and practice have shown us that a sense of camaraderie and greater cohesiveness develop when people perceive they face a common challenge and a common goal. This demands, though, that your employees see themselves, their managers, and the executives sharing in the work, the frustrations, the joys, and the pains of a difficult time.

It's not enough to say "We're all behind this new vision and new future" if your company still gives exclusive or hidden privileges to a few. Your workplace is a community, and you will strengthen this community—even in the worst of times—by spreading the perks widely, even those things usually reserved for just a few. Herb Baum, CEO and chair of The Dial Corporation, describes conversations with his people when he first came on board at Dial. "I learned," Baum recalls, "that employees were having to pay the company if they wanted to park under covered parking. Here in the desert, covered parking during the day is important. I couldn't fathom that the company charged people for coming to work." The practice of charging employees for the covered parking was stopped immediately. "There was no more assigned parking, you parked where you could whenever you got here. If parking isn't a perk for all employees, then it's not a perk for a select few."

If you lead an organization that still has executive bathrooms, prime parking spaces for managers, private elevators, and other symbols of privilege, now is a good time to eliminate these. Sure, some egos may be dented, but the respect you'll gain from employees will be tremendous. Work to create fewer signs of status and more signs of common living: open-door policies, access to information, greater transparency and fewer secret meetings, furnishings that are as comfortable in the break room as they are in corporate offices, even standards of dress that are more consistent across the levels and departments of your company.

Finally, when cuts must be made, take care that they are made equitably. You will arouse suspicion and discontent if only the lowest ranking people feel the brunt of an economic downturn, while senior managers and officers experience business as usual. Some leaders, such as those at Johnsonville Sausage, believe cuts start at the top. At Johnsonville, tough economic times mean that payroll cuts begin with the uppermost leaders and may never be directly felt by the lowest paid. The result? Extremely high levels of commitment from employees, and a greater willingness to help safely steer the company through hard times.

Recognize Others

There is plenty of talk about reward systems at work, from complex bonus structures to service pins and celebratory dinners. Yet in researching leaders whose organizations truly thrive during tough times, the focus instead is on simple, daily, spontaneous ways to recognize what people are doing.

During interviews at one insurance company, a technician described, "We have these monthly recognition dinners, but they just don't mean anything any more." The technician continued, "What we'd rather have is our director around to see what we're really doing, look us in the eye and say hello in the hallway, talk with us instead of to us, or say 'Thanks' and sound as if he meant it." People wanted to be recognized, in a simple, person-to-person way.

Recognition ceremonies can be an important part of work life, but not if they are perceived as a token acknowledgement of accomplishments. People want recognition—as a human being and as a member of the organization. It's a simple sign of respect. This is part of the reason why high participation workplaces are so successful—people feel like a recognized member of the organization.

With several hundred employees, Gary Bertch, of Bertch Cabinet Manufacturing, still makes it a point to learn new people's names, to introduce himself at their orientation sessions, and to come by their work areas to see how they are doing and if there is anything he can do to help. As he describes, "It's just common sense, I want to know the people I work with." Employees describe it as a sign of his respect for them. "People know Gary doesn't have to do that, that he's going out of his way to help them feel welcome and important to the company. I can't tell you how impressed I was when Gary came to my work area several weeks after I started, and he remembered my name!"

Knowing people and what they are doing means you can't lead from behind the closed door of your office (nor even from behind your open door). It demands management-by-walking-around, being highly visible and looking for what people are doing, asking what would help them be more effective, and serving as the resource that you are. This does not mean you want to stand and look over people's shoulders. It means knowing what's going on, what's needed, what's working, and what isn't. It means knowing who people are, or taking the time to find out. It means being a cheerleader some days, an architect others, and being personally involved always. And it's saying "thanks" with sincerity and specificity, and doing it in front of others.

Recognition takes many forms. It's the "Wall of Fame" in the break room, an article in the newspaper, a firm handshake, pizza, an afternoon off, or standing in line to get tickets for a movie your team wants to see. It's the company-wide celebration or a cup of cocoa when you arrive on a cold morning. It's having some fun. If you know your people, you'll know what will be meaningful to them. The key is to mix the ceremonies and rituals with spontaneous and unexpected actions that show you really do recognize and appreciate what people do. Pay attention, notice what people do, identify even the small milestones, and celebrate.

Opportunity for Friendship

Research has consistently shown over many years that when people work with those they view as friends, they are more likely to have higher job satisfaction, greater energy, and more creativity, and they are less likely to seek other employment. Unfortunately, many work cultures discourage friendship and social activities, believing they will lead to goofing off and reduced productivity. Even the ways in which we physically arrange work spaces can serve to unintentionally alienate people rather than encourage interaction.

Certainly we do not need to be best friends with everyone we work with. That's not the point. Work is a social activity, though—we need others to help us brainstorm, bounce ideas off of, challenge us, question our thinking, support us, and more. Leaders whose organizations thrive in tough times recognize the importance of simple and spontaneous relationships, and strive to organize work in a way that encourages such relationships. Many leaders also make sure there is ample opportunity outside of work for people to mix if they so choose.

Friendship with others does not thrive, however, in a rule-laden environment where people are fearful of doing something wrong, crossing a hidden boundary, or constantly wondering what the employee handbook would say. Instead, it requires as few formal rules and structures as possible, a reduction in hierarchy, and greater opportunity for self-organization and self-control. This way of conducting work encourages learning, development, and an attitude of critical thinking. It demands that people at work be treated as grown-ups. And it demands facility layouts that encourage people to gather in common areas. At companies like CarrAmerica, it's OK to hang out at the company coffee bar. They have, in fact, worked hard to shape the environment to fit the people rather than asking the people to adapt to their environment. As a result, productivity, creativity, innovation, informed risk-taking, and friendships are all high.

Management with a "Human Face"

In his book *Traditional Management and Beyond*, Omar Aktouf uses the phrase "managing with a human face" to describe a way of managing and leading that honors the human at work. While this seems like an obvious stand, it's one that too often gets set aside as we narrow our values to efficiency, profit margins, and productivity. We are surrounded by organizations that espouse, "Our people are our greatest asset," yet their policies, rules, and procedures fail to support such a value.

Managing with a human face means, simply, working as if people mattered—people in the workplace, in the community, and in the larger world. It does not require a charismatic personality or heroic actions. In fact, people involved in numerous research projects point to authenticity as being of far greater importance. This means dropping the trappings and distinctions of having a "business relationship" and interacting with all employees on a friendly basis. It means minimizing rules and eliminating signs of mistrust. Encourage people to make and learn from their mistakes without fear of punishment, shame, or retribution. It means not demanding that people ask permission to use the bathroom, and creating physical work conditions that are healthy and comfortable, even when there's no union to enforce this.

Trust, respect, and what has become known as empowerment are critical. Jim Lewis, president of Relationship Marketing, Inc., describes: "To me, this doesn't mean watching and overseeing new people until they have somehow earned our trust. I have to believe that people we hire are trustworthy and naturally empowered, right from the start. It's not something I or any other manager assigns to them." This sentiment is echoed by the people he employs. Says another member of Relationship Marketing, "Trust is assumed here. We're adults, and we're treated as adults, with all the freedoms and responsibilities that go with that."

Managing with a human face also means recognizing that people at work are whole people, more than a pair of hands, a knowledgeable mind, or a creative spirit that a company employs. Once again, we're surrounded by organizations that claim, "We hire the whole person." Yet if we look critically at many practices, we see vast discrepancies: excessive identification with a company is still encouraged, men and women alike risk losing their careers to attend their kids' baseball game or school play, or the insistence that 50- and 60-hour work weeks are part of "what work is" today.

Tough times at work demand more, not less, balance in our lives, where play, family, and leisure are as important—if not more so—than hard work and company profits. That's managing with a human face.

Make Some Fun

Humans are expressive beings, and having fun is a critical dimension of our creative energy. It involves living and working with spirit, humor, and joy and delight. During tough times, fun is even more important than ever. Without a sense of fun at work, our work becomes draining, deadening, meaningless.

Fun involves a deep sense of enjoyment and pleasure, a vitality of heart, mind, and soul. It asks us to work out loud and without fear. Fortunately, cultivating fun doesn't require an edict from management nor a large training budget. Recognizing others and celebrating those accomplishments are part of it. Being fully engaged in one's work is also fun, as is the chance to interact with others, debating, planning, sharing, arguing, laughing. Any way we refresh ourselves can be considered "fun."

We too often devalue novelty and playfulness at work, believing instead that work is serious business. We see this tendency, especially during difficult times when the focus is on survival. Yet playfulness and novelty are prime ways to break through the tension and seriousness we often feel during tough times, and often provide the very energy needed to overcome obstacles. It doesn't have to be outrageous (though sometimes that helps). Just stay open to silly or irreverent things.

Value the eccentric. Wear a clown nose (it's hard to take yourself too seriously when wearing one). Hold the next staff meeting at the zoo. Pay for lunch out—with the caveat that no one can discuss work or watch the time. Build a company playroom. Have the managers bring Popsicles to everyone on a hot day. Add new computer games or have a theme dress day. Remember: Novelty is a stimulus that triggers new associations, new perspectives, and new thinking.

Laughter is important, as the health field has demonstrated for many years, yet most adults don't do this nearly enough. Science is learning more and more about the value of laughter and its relationship with physical, mental, and spiritual well-being. Make it a central aspect of your organization's wellness, too. Lighten up! Be ready to laugh at yourself. Heaven knows there's lots of good material out there if we would just recognize the folly of much of what we do—just look at the rhetoric and jargon that passes today for workplace enlightenment. Re-learn curiosity, delight, and the art of foolishness.

Laughter and a sense of fun also help us to stop worrying about what others will think—and there's no greater killer of spirit than to dwell on what others might think of us. Stop looking around to see how you compare. Personally, as a work group, or as an organization, make your own decisions of what you want to be, how you want to look, the values you'll embrace and act upon, the benefits you'll offer, the schedule you'll establish, and the potentials you have. Forget what others might think, and do what is right within your work unit.

A final piece of making work fun is working as if people mattered. We've talked about this earlier. Don't be satisfied with having the words in the mission statement. Look more critically. Ask yourself, is the way we conduct work consistent with our belief that the people here matter? Take time every week to closely observe how work is organized and conducted: do your work processes, systems, and procedures back up your espoused values? Do a walk-your-talk audit.

What's fun? Having the room, power, and resources necessary to do and be something great!

Mel Brooks described, "...if you're alive, you got to flap your arms and legs, you got to jump around a lot, you got to make a lot of noise, because life is the very opposite of death....You've got to be noisy, or at least your thoughts should be noisy and colorful and lively." Find a way to break into the solemnity that may have crept into your work life. Having fun at work means living and working with passion, purpose, and intention—right out loud!

Energy Self-Assessment

Think about the following questions. On a sheet of paper, write out your responses and give detailed examples of specific actions you take that illustrate your answers.

1. Within my work group, are we really "all in this together," or do some people get hit harder than others when tough decisions are made?
2. During the tough times, do I make myself more, or less, accessible to others?
3. How effectively do I recognize the contributions that people make? Do I look people in the eye when we meet in the hallway, use a friendly tone when I'm talking, and find ways to celebrate even the small milestones we reach?
4. Do people here have a chance to develop friendships with others, both within and outside of their immediate work areas? Do I look for ways to increase the opportunity for interaction? Do we have at least one communal meeting area where we can gather informally?
5. Do I really "manage with a human face," or just go through the motions? Do I know peoples' names, know something about their lives, and do what I can to help them achieve a healthy balance of work, family, and leisure?

6. Do I look for ways to help make work fun for myself and others? Am I eager for novelty, or do I insist on doing things the same way every time?
7. Do I add to people's stress, or look for ways to reduce it?

On a scale of 1 to 10, with 1 being "Sadly Lacking" and 10 being "Outstanding," how would you rate yourself in terms of your ability to energize yourself and others at work?

Individual Reflection

Review your responses to the self-assessment. Circle the three items you would most like to change. Set your priorities. In Activity 6-1, write down five specific actions you can, and will, take to make these changes happen.

Activity 6-1. Priority Actions

1. ____________________

____

2. ____________________

____

3. ____________________

____

4. ____________________

____

5. ____________________

____

Group Reflection

Have other members of your work group or team complete a similar assessment on their own, rating either their own behavior or the climate within your work unit. Devote a staff meeting to discussing your answers, focusing on both the areas of agreement and the differences. Involve people in a probing conversation—where are we strongest in these areas? What might account for our different perceptions? Where do we need the most improvement? What matters to us? How can we really create a work climate and culture that energizes each one of us? Use this discussion to map out a plan for action that will help your unit maintain their energy and momentum. See Figure 6-1 for 30 ideas to re-energize work.

Figure 6-1. Climate-Builders—30 Ideas to Re-Energize Work

Value novelty . . . live out loud . . . work as if people mattered

- Conduct a field trip to another part of the organization
- Have a *real* brown bag lunch—go out on the lawn and enjoy getting away from the phones and computers
- Celebrate enthusiastically all birthdays, holidays, and special events
- Hold a story hour once a week for people to tell stories (personal or work) that are important to them
- Small pleasant surprises can be fun . . . have a chocolate break, or put a rose on every desk
- Buy tickets to a movie people want to see, and take an afternoon off to see it together
- Hold a *Most Improved Work Space* contest during National Clean Your Desk Week
- Create a play room, play corner, or other "sparkspace" for people to go to unwind, regroup, trigger new ideas, and think more creatively
- Create "real" job descriptions and job titles, rather than the more formalized ones we usually see
- Wear a clown nose around the company
- Have sponge sessions, where you take a walk and try to absorb as many new ideas as you can
- Put more color and texture in your work area
- Celebrate the best mistakes of the week
- Take regular Hunza Holidays (named for a tribe in Central Asia renowned for their health and longevity, who do nothing for five minutes of every hour)

Figure 6-1 (continued)

- Dance
- Hang an old, limp sock from the ceiling to remind you to relax
- Wear an unusual hat or costume
- Invent a new hobby
- Write all your team memos with crayons
- Have a snowball fight in the winter
- Surprise people by calling off work early for a day
- Sit on the floor for your meetings
- Meet once a month just to talk about what you value as a group
- Rollerblade in the hallway
- Meet for 15 minutes at the start of each day: have each person describe what they did yesterday, what's on today's agenda, and what others can do to help (no griping allowed)
- Conduct a personal walk-your-talk audit
- Hold a team pity party—put up sheets on the wall listing all the things that make your work life so miserable, then have everyone moan and groan over things for 30 minutes (**hint:** it doesn't take long for people to see just how ridiculous it all is)
- Look for ways to celebrate even the smallest successes . . . and make sure the rest of the company knows what your team does
- Be random and spontaneous . . . doing one thing regularly too often drains it of significance
- Be the kind of person you like to be around, and work as if people mattered

Chapter Seven: Ethics, Values, and Integrity

"In civilized life, law floats in a sea of ethics."
(Earl Warren)

The Rotarians had gathered for their weekly luncheon. A local pastor stood to say the invocation. Softly, he asked the group to stand and bow their heads. "God," he began, "let us live by the same values we want our children to have."

Realtor Bill Weier said, "Ouch!" even before the "Amen."

Banker Ed Burke turned to the pastor and said, "You sure know how to hurt a guy."

Table talk for the rest of the lunch focused on ethics and values and integrity: Topics like what a person would and wouldn't do, and where the line gets drawn. Do people have one set of values for personal life and another for business? And is honesty a matter of numbers? "Do big dollars make it easier to lie than just a few?" someone asked. Or does the size of the event have nothing to do with honesty.

In a central Arizona city, a high school senior failed her final test in a course and was told she wouldn't graduate the next week. For the previous six weeks, she and her parents had been advised she had failing grades and wouldn't graduate unless the grades improved. She had earlier been disciplined for plagiarizing a term paper.

When the girl was told she wouldn't graduate because she flunked the course, her parents sued. The lawyer, in his letter to the teacher, threatened to bring out all of her past classroom dealings, her own education, her teaching style, all of her previous grading systems, her personal friendships, and on and on and on. It was a very intimidating letter. The teacher didn't back down.

But the school board caved in. The girl graduated. The next week, some of her friends went back to summer school to complete courses they had not passed. This one girl had the summer free. The press had a hey-day with all the events.

Three Important Words

Ethics. Values. Integrity. So what are they? And what are yours? Was the teacher ethical? Did the parents show integrity? Was the school board living out its values?

According to the *Random House Webster's College Dictionary*, ethics are the moral principles or rules of conduct that govern a particular person, group, or culture. The study of ethics is the branch of philosophy that deals with values relating to human conduct, with respect to right and wrong.

Values are the abstract concepts of what is right and wrong, and what is worthwhile and desirable. Values are the principles or standards of conduct. Values are what ethics are all about. Values are what drive our actions.

Integrity is the uncompromising adherence to ethical principles.

Here's a way to put them together in one sentence so that they make sense: Ethics are our principles of conduct, based upon our values; and integrity is our ability to consistently live by our expressed values.

In this chapter, we want to show you ways to think through your own value system. Remember, though, that this isn't a book on business ethics, or corporate responsibility, or even personal values. Ethics, however, are important for being an effective leader in tough times. Since the collapse of Enron, ethics are talked about again in the boardroom, cafeteria, and elevator. It is increasingly difficult to lead in tough times if you're not aware of your own basic values and ethics.

How Did We Get to This Point in U.S. History?

Before going any further, let's stop and think about how we got to this point in history. In a 2002 editorial, *Business Week* magazine calls the recent charges against some corporate leaders, the "corporate crime wave." It will get worse, they predict. It has become so flagrant that Vanguard Mutual Fund founder John C. Bogie and Warren E. Buffett have started a shareholder rights group. "What communism could not do," (destroy capitalism) activist Ralph Nader wrote, "the big business bosses are doing to the market system and the financial industry."

Confidence in corporate America is at an all-time low. People are selling stocks, taking a loss now, because they believe if they hold on to certain stocks the losses will be even greater. The confidence has become so eroded that corporations whose stock sold in the $50s or even $100s a few months ago are selling for just a few dollars today.

How did we get to the point where executives falsify corporate financial reports and where auditors shred documents relating to a criminal case? How did we get to the point where…

- Consumer confidence in corporate leadership is nil?
- Trust in the stock market is down the tubes?
- CEO income is now 400 to 500 times what the average worker makes, up from 70 times in 1985?
- Top executives inflate earnings so that the shares go up and they can unload them before the truth is known?
- U.S. companies can move out of the country to avoid paying U.S. taxes?
- Auditors cook the books, and tell their clients how to hide losses?
- Corporate officers, like feudal barons, can pillage their companies, leaving the serfs to starve?
- Retired people lose their retirement incomes because a few executives stuff their pockets with millions of dollars of invested funds?
- College students, in a course on ethics, are caught cheating on the final exam?
- Even church affiliated money managers pocket millions, cook the books, and let thousands of trusting retirees go without healthcare because they no longer have any retirement income?

Maybe it began when we looked the other way while someone took a few paper clips home from the office—maybe even a ream of copy paper for their home printer. Or maybe it began when parents laughed when their kid stuck a candy bar in their coat pocket and walked out of the store. Or maybe it began when we thought that talking with our kids about values and ethics wasn't cool.

How it started isn't really important right now. Of more importance are the values and morals held by leaders.

What Are Your Values?

Is stuffing a candy bar into your pocket and walking out of the store immoral? Is stuffing your pocket with shareholder's money through cooking the books unethical? Sure, lots of people as kids stuffed a candy bar into their pockets and walked out of the store.

"But that's different," we say. Maybe it is. Or maybe it isn't.

Is it unethical to put your company's operation in Bermuda, even though most of your business is within the United States, just to avoid paying U.S. taxes? It may be legal, but to many of us, it also is against our value system. It's not right, not pulling your share.

Is it unethical to tell a customer their order will be in Tuesday, when you know it will be at least Thursday, and maybe even Friday? Or is that just good customer retention? Is a salary 200 times that of the average salary of your employees good business? Bad policy? Or maybe just "not right."

Is it unethical to pay a CEO a big bonus, while the company is thinking about bankruptcy? At a 2002 senate hearing, Senator Byron Dorgan objected to a payout to ousted Qwest chief Joseph P. Nacchio. "When somebody runs a company into the ground, you don't give them a $10 million bonus," Dorgan said. Qwest President Afshin Mohebbi defended the payout as legal.

It may be legal, but is it moral or ethical?

Business columnist Jon Talton recently asked a similar series of questions.

> "What do these actions have to do with corporate wrongdoing? Everything.
>
> "Taken together they are its dirty seedbed of self-dealing, insider privilege, lying, fraud, and continued contempt for the suckers who are the average taxpayers."

Obviously Talton doesn't think much of many of today's corporate leaders. Particularly those who led to the fall of Enron and WorldCom, and the fraudulent practices of Xerox and Arthur Andersen.

"Theodore Roosevelt called such behavior 'crimes of astute corruption,'" Talton adds.

Only a few years ago not much would have been said about an isolated case. But 2001 and 2002 saw so many examples of executive suite fraud that people—stockholders—are calling for a whole new sense of ethics and fair play in the business sector.

There are those who resist cleansing laws that mandate hard time (incarceration) for leaders who approve the kind of practices that led to the fall of Enron, WorldCom, and many others—who seek for less executive accountability than now. They're often called lobbyists. Some are called legislators. But Washington, D.C., attorney Charles Goldman believes, "Post-Enron will be tough on executives and corporate boards. It's a whole new ball game."

So what are your values? What do you consider to be moral? Right? Wrong?

Instead of the lack of ethics becoming more rampant, maybe this is the time for real leaders to show that basic values of right and wrong still impact on how things get done. After all, every decision we make as leaders, every action we take as leaders, is based on our consciously—or unconsciously—held ethics.

Here are some workplace examples people have reported to us. As you read each example, ask yourself, "What would I do? What do I think is ethical? Moral? Right? Wrong?"

Is it OK to . . . and why or why not?

- Take home pens and pencils and paper clips from the office?
- Use the company car for personal business?
- Use the company credit card for dinner with the family?
- Make your assistant stay late to complete a report because you forgot it had to be done and you have tickets to the baseball game?
- Shout and call one of your team members names because she didn't do something the way you thought it ought to be done?
- Have two sets of books?
- Incorporate in a foreign country so that you don't have to pay U.S. taxes?
- "Accidentally" slip your hand over the breasts of an attractive female subordinate?
- Reduce the quarterly dividend so that the company can "loan" you several million dollars?

The surest way to keep your picture off the front page of the business section is to do what's right, what's moral, what's ethical—to act as if those things mattered.

Thinking Through What's Right, Moral, and Ethical

If you're like many Americans, life goes on without much thought about values and ethics. We live out each day doing what seems to come easily and—sometimes—naturally. Sure, once in a while we stop and think about it. But by and large we make decisions, interact with people, drive home after work, relate with our neighbors, buy groceries, talk with the kids, and interact with our significant other without much thought about ethics. We just do it.

So, what do you really value? Consider to be moral? Right? Wrong? Immoral?

Who Are Your Heroes?

To get you started thinking about your ethical values, pull out a sheet of paper and draw a line down the center. On the left side, write "Heroes." On the right side, write "Values." Fold the paper in half so that you see only one column at a time.

First, make a list of the people you admire—heroes. These people can be personal friends or family, alive or deceased, famous or unknown, wealthy or poor, or whatever. The only criterion is that you admire these people, for whatever reason. These are your personal heroes. Make the list as long as you want. You'll probably have at least ten names. Hopefully more.

Now unfold your paper. On the right column, start to add what it is about each person you've listed that you admire. Make your list detailed. Don't leave anything out. If you need more room to write, grab another sheet of paper.

When you're finished, set the paper out in front of you. Stare at it.

Just let your eyes wander from word to word.

Then start writing a list of what's important to you: your values, ethics, morals—the things that guide your decisions.

It's a common belief that what you admire in others, you also admire in yourself.

But be cautious. Just because you admire one person doesn't mean you have that quality yourself in the same intensity as the person you consider a hero. Abe Lincoln may have had a willingness to act on deep belief to the level of 10, while someone else who admires Lincoln, only lives out that quality to a level of 5 or 6.

But if you admire it, you have it. And you push it to a higher level by living it.

As an example, Figure 7-1 lists Richard's heroes with a very brief description of the values and qualities he admires in each person. Some are famous. Most are not. Some he knew (no, Richard is old, but he never met Ben Franklin).

Figure 7-1. People Richard Admires—And Why

Heroes	Admires These Values, Qualities
1. Howard Deems, my father	1. Honest, sensible, a leader, sense of integrity—did what was right, not what was expedient.
2. Abraham Lincoln	2. Stood up for what he believed, even though not easy or popular.
3. Samuel Deems, my grandfather	3. An adventurer; headed west as a young man, with only time, energy, and dreams.
4. Bill Pfieff, high school football coach	4. Believed in people, worked you hard, but was fair, pushed you to new heights.
5. Eleanor Roosevelt	5. Worked hard to help people have better lives, more concerned about people than what others thought about her.
6. Buzz Hargleroad, cousin	6. Put his own life in danger for what he believed.
7. Martin Luther King, Jr.	7. Used his great abilities to help a nation come to terms with racism.
8. Dick Cavett	8. Worked very hard to bring his dreams to reality. Determination.
9. Marion Marsh Brown, my aunt	9. Became a widely recognized author of historical novels, encouraged me to write.
10. Benjamin Franklin	10. Innovator, always thinking outside the box, knew how to get things done.

As you look at Richard's list, you understand that he values integrity, accomplishments, standing up for what one believes, and caring. His ethics, his beliefs, are all inherent within each of the qualities of the people he admires. And if you pushed him, he could add a great deal of detail for each hero.

Heroes are good. They can serve as role models and remind us of what we are capable of being.

Take time to identify your heroes, and why they are your heroes. When you complete the activity, you will have a much deeper, clearer appreciation for what's important to you—your values, your ethics—so that you can live with integrity.

What would you do with your time?

Here's another action to help you think through your values. Imagine you have just won the lottery. You have enough money for the rest of your life, and you don't need to work for hire anymore. In fact, you *can't* work at a job that pays a salary. What would you do with your time? After you've gone around the world and done all the traveling that you want to do, how will you fill your days and nights? Take time to think through what you would do—and why.

Figure 7-2 shows how Terri would spend her time.

Figure 7-2. Terri Would Spend Her Time…

If I didn't have to work any more for money, this is how I'd spend my time…

- Become active in groups concerned with social justice.
- Find people who struggle to get through their life and whose lives I could help to make easier with financial assistance. Help them to focus less on survival and more on their potential.
- Pursue grass-roots projects and initiatives.

How you would spend your time says a lot about what you value, what you consider right or wrong, and your own personal system of ethics.

It's Not Always Black or White

Wouldn't it be great if decisions were easy? Black and white? No-brainers? You didn't have to think about the decision or action because it was so obviously either the right or wrong thing to do?

Ain't so.

As leaders, we're often called on to make decisions when the ethical issues are blurred, not clear, not black and white, but rather shades of gray. It's a little bit right, but then it's also a little bit wrong. And you often have to do some serious thinking about how to handle many situations. "Ethics are fluid in this society," reminds pharmacist manager Steve Kastendiek, RPh. It's easier to deal with touchy situations when you've already spent some time and energy thinking about your own principles and ethics—like making a list of your heroes.

Here's an exercise that will make you stretch. It's called Alligator River, and some attribute its origin to the *David Frost Show.* As you read the story, think about the actions, and ethics, of each of the characters. At the end, you'll be asked to identify who you think was the most moral. Enjoy dealing with the questions.

Once upon a time there was a woman named Abigail who was in love with a man named Gregory. Unfortunately, they lived on opposite sides of a large river filled with alligators. The river was teaming with angry, people-eating alligators who would line the shores waiting for someone to try to cross or fall in.

Abigail wanted to cross the river to be with Gregory, as she often did. But the bridge had washed out in last week's rain. They could look at each other from opposite shores, but they couldn't talk and could not touch.

Abigail went to talk with Sinbad who had a strong, safe, riverboat. She asked Sinbad to take her across the river so that she could be with Gregory. He said he'd be glad to, if she would consent to go to bed with him the night before the voyage. Abigail refused.

She went to her mother, Martha, to explain her dilemma. Martha said it was a tough decision, but Abigail was an adult and had to make her own decisions. And besides, she didn't want to be involved at all in this situation. Feeling there was no other way, Abigail accepted Sinbad's terms. The next morning Sinbad fulfilled his promise and delivered her to the arms of Gregory.

When she told Gregory about her agreement to cross the river, he cast her aside in anger. Heartsick and dejected, Abigail turned to Slug who lived by the river and told him all that had happened. Slug, feeling compassion for Abigail, found Gregory and beat him up. Abigail was overjoyed at the sight of Gregory getting his due. As the sun sets, we see Abigail laughing at Gregory.

- Interesting story, isn't it. Now here's the tough part.
- Five characters: Abigail, Gregory, Martha, Sinbad, and Slug.
- Who's the most moral? And why?
- Rank the characters in Activity 7-1.

Activity 7-1. Character Ranking

Write down your own ranking and why you rank each person the way you do.

1. Most moral ______________________________
2. Next ______________________________
3. Next ______________________________
4. Just about the least moral ______________________________
5. Least moral ______________________________

If you want to add to the depth and frustration of this exercise, gather some friends or co-workers together. Tell the story. Ask them to rank-order the characters and be ready to defend their ranking. Then let the discussion begin. It will be emotional. It will be deep. People will see what others value. And you'll learn some things about yourself and about others.

But It's Not Always Just a Story

Sometimes you have a situation that seems as hopeless as the Alligator River. There are many issues involved, and it's not easy to decide what's the best action. Often, none of the options are what you want and you're faced with an ethical dilemma. But they're the options you have to deal with. When you put energy into clarifying what you believe, it will be easier to make your decision when it's shades of gray. And you will be asked to make many decisions that might be in conflict with what you believe.

Values

The exercises above are designed to help you think through your values and make them clearer. It's part of the process of valuing, and the theoretical constructs go back to John Dewey and Louis Raths. The process involves seven actions.

PRIZING one's beliefs and actions:

1. Prizing and cherishing what one believes, being proud of one's personal values.
2. Letting others know, when appropriate, what it is that a person values and prizes and is willing and not willing to do.

CHOOSING one's beliefs and behaviors

3. Choosing from alternatives, knowing that there are other value options one can hold.
4. Choosing values after thinking through the consequences of each value.
5. Being free to choose one's values, unencumbered by family restrictions, value systems of others, value systems imposed by other people or organizations.

ACTING on one's beliefs

6. Acting out one's values and making decisions based on one's values.
7. Acting out one's values with consistency, and repetition so that people who know you know how you will act in certain situations.

When you've completed the several exercises above, sit back and think through what you've come up with. And then congratulate yourself. You have been involved in the process of valuing.

Basic Ethical Principles

In a recent survey of a library's section on business leadership, nearly every book examined had something to say about ethics and values.

Ethical principles were held up as being necessary for economies to effectively function. Without ethics, there could be no investing, no trusted commerce, nor any exchange of monies or goods.

Here are seven basic ethical principles for you to think about. We believe they are basic for leading in tough times.

1. *The leader is honest.* There is no leadership without an unswerving commitment to honesty. The leader is trusted to be honest: honest in profit predictions, honest in actual compensation, honest in every interaction with employees, shareholders, and the public. Because of this unswerving honesty, people trust the leader to say what she/he means and mean what she/he says. Without basic trust between leader and follower, the leader is forever suspect.

2. *The leader does not take advantage of others.* Fairness and respect is the foundation of all personal and organizational relationships. Just because you know how to cook the books and deceive the stockholders, doesn't mean you will do it. Just because you know the person beneath you will do all that you ask, doesn't make it right. Not taking advantage of others is part of a leader's basic ethical system.

3. *The leader does not intentionally discriminate, hurt, or demean another person.* There is intrinsic worth in being human, in existing. It doesn't make any difference about a person's gene pool, skin color, language, or status. The leader does nothing to intentionally negatively impact another person.

4. *The leader takes responsibility for his/her actions.* In other words, the leader is accountable. He or she doesn't blame others for his or her errors, or lack of attention, or not keeping track of what's going on. There's a segment of lawmakers who are pushing for increased legal accountability of leaders. "If they won't be responsible for their actions out of a sense of doing what's right, then we'll pass laws to make them accountable," stated one lawmaker.

5. *The leader asks others to work and live with an informed and shared value system.* The leader is not afraid to tell someone that their values are in conflict, and knows how to share his/her values in a way that invites the other person to also choose similar values. The leader is ready to walk away from someone

who asks a person to do something that is blatantly contrary to one's ethics.

6. *The leader has integrity.* People can count on the leader being consistent in living out his or her values. The leader is trustworthy. You trust what the leader says because the person shows a consistent pattern of ethical actions.

7. *When faced with a conflict of values, the leader analyzes and evaluates the facts, and makes the decision.* Five questions the leader asks when trying to solve a moral issue include:

   - What benefits and what harms will each possible course of action produce, and which alternative will lead to the best overall results?
   - What moral rights do the involved parties have, and which course of action best respects these rights?
   - Which course of action treats everyone the same, except where there is a morally justifiable reason not to, and does not show favoritism or discrimination?
   - Which course of action advances the common good, or promotes principles of unity and justice?
   - Which course of action develops ethical virtues?

Unfortunately for leaders, there is often not a single, automatic solution for every event. To be a real leader in tough times, the leader must be aware of his or her values, what the person believes is right or wrong, and then work very hard to live with integrity. Steve Kastendieck puts it this way: "At the end of the day I ask myself, 'Did I do some good today? Did I bring something to my work group that wasn't there before I got there, or wouldn't be there if I left?'"

We think that's ethical leadership in action.

* * *

"I would rather be the man who bought the Brooklyn Bridge than the man who sold it."

(Will Rogers)

Section Two: Leaders in Action

"A good company delivers excellent products and services; a great one delivers excellent products and services and strives to make the world a better place."
(Bill Ford—Chairman and CEO, Ford Motor Company)

Chapter Eight: How Do I Lead Others Through Change?

The World Future Society projects there will be more change in this decade than in the past 200 years! And in the past 200 years, we've seen the development of railroads, automobiles, airplanes, the Internet, ballpoint pens, cell phones, angioplasties, and microwave popcorn.

And that's just a sample.

- The half-life of an engineer's knowledge today is only five years.
- In electronics, fully half of what a student learns as a freshman is obsolete by the person's senior year.
- By 2005, China could have as many as 85 million people online.
- There is more computing power in our handheld dual band cell phones than in the first computer WorkLife Design used in 1982.
- Over 10 percent of workers under age 30 are trying to start their own businesses.

How's all that for change? If you and your organization are not in the midst of some kind of change project, you will be by the end of the year. Or you won't exist.

Leading others in the tough times of change can be challenging. But we've learned from mistakes, and from others, what it takes to make change work. Here are the six actions it takes to thrive on the question mark of what's changing next.

1. Put Change into Perspective

For over 50 years, we've been taught that people "naturally resist change" and that we are supposed to resist it. And that whenever you change anything within an organization, your people will resist it. We think that's bunk. It's a myth that's simply not true. All you have to do is stop and examine human existence to realize we thrive on change.

When you stop and examine your life, you realize you have run toward most change! Who of us did not, figuratively, run toward learning how to read, learning how to tie our own shoes, getting our driver's license, experiencing our first kiss, staying out all night, or getting the big promotion? Each of those actions was the beginning of major change. It doesn't make sense to say that we resist change when we realize we have reached out for most of it.

Of course it doesn't mean we like all the change that comes our way. Richard wasn't jumping up and down with excitement while waiting on the gurney for his first angioplasty. But even as he lay there wondering what was coming next, his inner self was telling him to run toward health—to make it work.

The most common experience of us all since birth has been change: changing bodies, changing weather, changing moods, changing fads, changing foods—change. Which is why it's difficult to believe that people naturally resist change. What a cruel hoax to play on humankind: living with continual change, but hard wired to resist it. Common sense tells us that we run toward most change and that our natural striving is to make it work—to deal with it.

What you believe about change makes a big difference. It has an impact on all that we do. For example, if you believe change is bad, and you're supposed to resist it, how will that belief impact on your children? You will strive to keep them from change, won't you? But did you do this? Probably not. You helped them learn how to read. To safely cross the street by themselves. To get ready for that first real job. In other words, you helped them run toward change.

"When I lost my job," states insurance executive Tom Van Fossen, "I took a few hours to feel sorry for myself. And then I did the only thing I could. I started running toward change. I started running toward those changes that would put me in a position where I could be successful. That's my basic instinct."

Did we run toward the events of 9/11? Of course not! But have you ever seen a nation, a people, strive so hard to come together, support each other, and foster healing?

Here's what we know about change.

Self-chosen change is the easiest. Change that we've been involved in designing is typically change that we support. Change that's foisted upon us from outside sources is change that might not have our full support. It doesn't mean we resist it; it just means we might not get behind it. This is one reason why involving your people in creating the change helps ensure their support.

Change that affects relationships is the most difficult change. That's why death of a parent, spouse, sibling, or good friend is so difficult. It affects our relationships. That's also why a divorce is often so difficult for many people. The relationships are different. Life is different. And it's not always easy. Underneath, however, is the striving to deal with it—and make it work.

Breaking a habit is not the same as resisting change. Habits are things we do automatically so that we don't have to think about them. If we don't have to think about them, there's extra energy to deal with other things. But learning how to fold your arms in a way differently than you usually do has nothing to do with resisting change. It does, however, have a lot to do with the power of a habit. Some organizational change deals with having to break old habits, like coming to work at a different time. But most organizational change has to do with the way we do things.

We are what we are because of change. Think about it: The impact of change in our lives has had great impact on our development as people. This doesn't mean we always like it. But it does mean change molds us. For example, Richard's father suddenly died at one of the lowest points in Richard's life: He had been terminated and had been without a job for nearly a year. He had gone through a divorce. And then, the elder Dr. Howard Deems died. Richard's father didn't get to see him take a position at a major university, or have his first book published. But the experience changed the way Richard views family and relationships and time. It was one experience that shaped him.

Our belief about change impacts the people around us. If we believe people are supposed to resist change, then that's what we will expect from others. And they will. If we believe that people run toward most change, they will probably strive to meet our expectation. It applies to us, also. Afraid of asking too much of our people, we often ask too little of ourselves.

The first step for leading others through change is to put change into perspective and acknowledge that people do not naturally resist change. We may not like it all, but our natural striving is to make it work. Explore the impact of your beliefs in Activity 8-1.

Activity 8-1. Explore the Impact of Your Beliefs

I want my basic belief about change to be...

____

____

____

____

And it will have these kinds of impacts on...

____

____

The people I work with...

____

____

My boss... ______________________________

____

____

My family... ____________________________

____

____

____

2. Celebrate the Ways You Strive to Make Change Work

Ever notice the different ways people around you react to change? You'll quickly notice they don't all react the same way. Some people support change only after a lot of thought—maybe even their own research. And then there are those who jump first, and then look to see if there's anything on the other side. They seem to be outside the box all the time. Sometimes, you wonder if they even know there is a box.

"Nobody naturally resists change," states best-selling author Kathy Kolbe. Kolbe re-discovered the concept of conation, or natural strengths, which had been studied in earlier decades. "We all have instincts, the natural way in which we strive to get things done," Kolbe asserts. "Once we know our MO, *modus operendi,* we understand the kinds of information and structure we need to make change work for us, and how we will naturally take action to make change happen," Kolbe adds. Natural strengths are divided into four Conative Action Modes®: Fact Finder, Follow Thru, Quick Start, and Implementer (think of a farm implement, a tool).

The Fact Finder instinct is the striving to gather information—to ask why. Without the rationale for any kind of organizational change, people with high levels of Fact Finder energy will get stressed. "They need information, the what, why, and how," adds Will Rapp, President of Kolbe Corp. International. "Otherwise, the lack of information is stressful."

If you work with people who have a lot of natural energy in the Fact Finder mode, they need lots of information before they can support change. They need the "why" behind the change. Why is it necessary? Why this change and not another? Why at this time and not sometime else? Give them the information they need for buy-in, and they will fully support the change. Without the information, they may or may not get behind it. It's not that they're resisting change—you just haven't provided the in-depth information they need to support it.

And the information needs to be both verbal and written. Tell them about the change and give them a white paper on the change. Why it's necessary, who was involved in creating it, what the results should be, how it will affect them, and so on. Give Fact Finders the printed explanation and an opportunity to ask clarifying questions. Without this information, they will most likely have all kinds of reasons why the change won't work.

The Follow Thru instinct needs to know the new structure, what and when things will be different. And how their routine will be changed. "Once I had my time line of what changes were to take place, and when," states operations officer Leigh Lewis, "the change was a breeze. No intense times. No going home tired at night." Without knowing what was to take place, and when, Lewis would have been stressed, dragging her feet, and seeming to "resist" the change.

As you lead others through change, you will probably have a number of people with a lot of energy in the Follow Thru action mode, like Lewis. They need information. But they need it in the form of a chart. What will take place this week, next week, the week after. They need a schedule, a time line, and an organized way to get things done. They need to know how their daily routine will be the same or different.

People with a high level of energy in both Fact Finder and Follow Thru need the information *before* the change takes place. And they need time to think about it, ask questions, and think through in their own minds how they will function. If you give these Fact Finders and Follow Thrus the word on Monday that things will change on Tuesday, you will have lots of heel dragging. They won't support you. It's not that they are resisting change. It's that you have not given them what they need in order to support the change.

The Quick Start mode is the instinct to innovate. People with a high level of energy in Quick Start naturally juggle many things at one time and come up with the new approach, new ways of doing things. "This is the person who thrives on change," Kolbe adds, "and if there isn't enough change happening, they will go out and create it for themselves." The Quick Start instinct is the instinct to ask, "Why not?"

A person with a lot of energy in Quick Start needs to be involved in creating the change. They are the ones who naturally brainstorm, think outside the box, and come up with lots of ideas. People with this natural talent are the ones who often drive change. However, when they're not involved in creating the change, they might not support it. Or they might quietly sulk in their own work area, or find activities outside the organization where they can be involved in creating new directions.

The Implementer action mode is the instinct to physically demonstrate or work with machines or tools. "People with high energy in the Implementer mode need to take action by working with their hands, being physical, and are drawn to the out of doors," Kolbe states. This is the person who understands what they can see or touch. Words are not as important as pictures or a model. They will ask if the quality of the product they produce will be altered, or if they will still have quality equipment to use, or if they will finally get equipment upgrades.

People with strengths in the Implementer action mode don't get excited about a change if it's only announced through a wordy memo. They will ask for a diagram, or a 3-D model. And as they look at the model, the change will begin to make sense.

The research at WorkLife Design shows that when people don't have the kinds of information they need, according to their natural strengths or MO, they'll hold back getting involved. But when people have the kind of information they need about change that makes sense, they support it and make it work. And then everybody can celebrate the new direction.

3. Show Your People How to Create Their Future

The best way to predict your future is to create it. And here is a way you can involve your people in creating their organizational future.

Over the years, our research at WorkLife Design indicates many employee groups go through organizational change in a common pattern. Surrounding this pattern of behaviors are rumors. A fairly common reaction pattern is shown in Figure
8-1.

There are always rumors—some are accurate, and some not. Once the announcement is made, things begin to happen very quickly. First there is Positioning, as people jockey for position as to who will influence the group's reaction. People will be vying to influence the group to view the announced change with enthusiasm, hesitation, anger, or wait-and-see.

Confusion follows very quickly. There are questions about who does and does not have power, where the decisions are coming from, what will be the effects on others, and what does it all mean for the long term.

Figure 8-1. Reaction Pattern

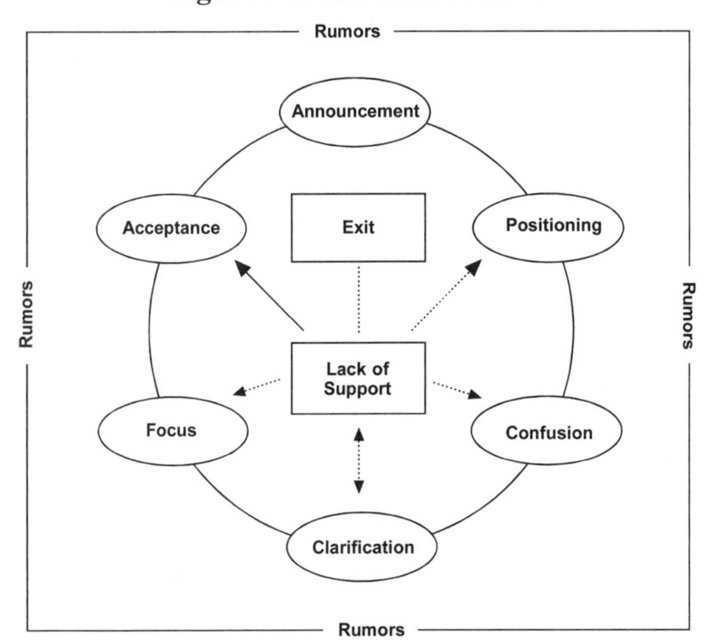

Depending on how smart the leadership is, Clarification either follows quickly or takes time. If it takes too long, the morale of the group plummets, and the organization may be in serious trouble. Clarification is when people's questions are answered, it becomes more clear what the new direction means and how it will impact on people, and the new direction of the work unit is defined. Since no leader can anticipate all reactions, clarification is also the time when planning mistakes are corrected.

Focus is when the direction and new goals are clear and people know what's expected and where the work group is going. Acceptance is when people accept the change, either with enthusiasm, or wait-and-see, or sometimes even with indifference.

The dotted lines show that at most every point people have an option to drag their feet and not support the change. They will then either Exit or return to one of the Cycle's stages.

In our workshops on change management, we involve people in discussing the illustration and what they have experienced in their work unit. We even ask them to come up with their own diagram. We've had roller coasters, flow charts, pinwheels, and even a Christmas tree.

Here comes the real power of this exercise. After people have discussed for ten minutes or so how their work unit has been reacting to change, we shift the assignment. We ask them to discuss, and illustrate, how they WANT their work unit to react to future change. We're not interested in how they have been reacting to change. We want them to create their futures, and you begin that process by having people discuss how they want things to happen in the future.

We have seen many "ah-hahs" during this exercise. We have also seen, as people go through their discussions and drawing, shifts in their mindsets and eventually, their workplace culture. It's as if the people are given permission to create their future behavior, which is, indeed, what the exercise does.

There are three more steps. First, the group needs to do a gap analysis between how they want things to be and how it is now. They need to list, in detail, the skills and competencies they need in order to react to future change the way they want to.

Second, the group needs to identify the ways they will gain the competencies to react to future change the way they want to. Now you have the leadership development program outlined, in a good amount of detail. You can approach the same work from an appreciative perspective, as well: What are the instances when the ideal is being reached? And what steps can be taken to help make this happen more often?

Third, you need to build in some process to continue reviewing their shared vision, and ensuring that it is becoming reality. Without this planned follow-through, there might be lots of great ideas, but not much ever happens. If not much happens, people will revert to their old ways of dragging their heels. Instead, make use of the ideas and wisdom of your people.

4. Manage the Intense Times

As you lead others through the tough times of major change, there will be times that are intense, stressful, and uptight. Often there is too much in too little time, and people get stressed. Leaders get stressed, too. Acknowledge that you and your people will have those kinds of days. And get ready to deal with them.

"The most effective way to manage your stress," states wellness advisor Debbie Harper, "is to release your endorphins." Endorphins: Those magical chemicals that your body releases. Endorphins make us feel good, take away pain, increase our energy, and fight depression.

"The single best way to release your endorphins is through exercise," Harper counsels. It can be walking outdoors, walking on a treadmill, hiking, jogging, lifting weights, dancing. "But it takes 20 minutes of exercise to begin the endorphin flow," Harper acknowledges.

Listening to music, many people report, also releases endorphins. What kind of music? It varies widely. Some like soft music, or new age, or classical. During a career change workshop in Miami, one person said she relaxed by listening to heavy metal. Her favorite? Iron Butterfly's "Inna Godda da Vida." Take time to explore the music that releases your endorphins. And then enjoy.

So you don't want to just listen? Do you want to get involved? Great! Singing, reports Case Western Reserve University professor of surgery Richard Fratianne, relaxes people, eases pain, and may even speed recovery. Researchers around the world are using music to help heal people. Burn victims are encouraged to sing while their dressings are being changed. It reduces pain. Cancer patients who listen to music and even improvise on instruments see the level of their stress hormones drop.

Making music is a great way to deal with the intense times. It gives you more energy to make change work.

Laughter is still another way to relax, reduce your stress, and release those feel-good endorphins. It's strong medicine, researchers have learned. Over the past 30 years, there have been many studies that show the power of laughter.

"Laughter is a powerful antidote to stress," states University of California professor Lee Berk. His research shows that watching and laughing at a funny video decreases two key stress hormones. And Stanford University professor emeritus William Fry found that laughing increases blood flow and contracts muscles. It's a mini-workout.

Many people report that laughter is what keeps them going—watching funny movies, watching old Johnny Carson shows, watching whatever it is that makes them laugh. Training manager Sam Stevens reports that he gets on the treadmill every morning at 5:15 a.m. As he walks, he watches a funny sitcom. "By the time I've done 30 minutes and laughed out loud several times," he reports, "I'm ready to tackle anything that comes my way."

There are many other ways to handle stress. Getting involved with a volunteer project gets a person thinking about things besides self. Pets relieve a great deal of stress. Talking it out is yet another way. For some reason, it does more good to hear yourself say, "Gee I'm stressed," than to just think it. Forget the six-pack approach, though. When a person is stressed, it is not the time to do lots of drinking. In fact, it's the time to reduce drinking.

You may want to provide some training for your people in how to handle the intense times. We've learned over the years, though, that when told they were going to have "Stress Training" people assumed they were supposed to be stressed. If they weren't stressed, they got stressed.

Instead, we prefer to talk about managing the intense times. Changing a few words makes it more clear: there will be times that are described as "intense," and here are ways to manage it. Prepare your people to deal with the intense times, and look for ways to re-energize people at work.

5. Practice the Art of Continual Change

There has always been change. And the pace of change will accelerate. The key words for high performance organizations have been, and will continue to be, continual change. To be successful in leading others through change, you will need to show people the skills to thrive in the midst of continual change. It can be done.

View Change as Opportunity

A few years ago, Richard was conducting a life/career planning workshop in Kansas City. The discussion had turned to change, and how it's sometimes just plain hard work to make a successful career change.

During a break, a woman came up to him. "Think of it as CEO," she said. "Think of what as CEO?" he asked. "Change," came her quick reply. "I look at it this way—if you want to be CEO of your own life, then think CEO. Change Equals Opportunity!"

Then she went on to talk about all the opportunities she had uncovered in the midst of every major change she experienced. She talked about being caught in a downsizing. Rather than a disaster, she reported, the event was full of unexpected opportunities.

She scrunched family finances, went back to school, and began a new career as a budget analyst. That opened the door for a new job with a smaller, growing company, who liked her years of work experience—an opportunity.

In fact, there were lots of opportunities. Her kids got into the habit of pitching in and taking care of chores around the house while she studied at night. One night a week the family made sure they were all home at the same time for meals together and family time.

While the woman shared her story, a slightly balding man listened intently. "I did something similar," he injected. "Except I didn't have a rallying cry, like CEO, to guide me through it all," the man added. Then he began to tell his story.

A promotion took him to a new city. Kind of shy, he had a difficult time actively meeting his new co-workers and really getting acquainted with his new boss. Then one weekend he began to make a list of the pluses and minuses of this new assignment. "I made a really long list of what wasn't right," he added, "and then I started working on the pluses." The man realized the change had brought lots of new opportunities. He had become re-invigorated about his work. He liked what he was doing, and he liked the few people he knew within the company.

To fill free time, he started running every morning. "It wasn't long before I had more energy than I'd had for over 10 years," he said. His marriage was more satisfying. He spent time talking with his kids who had scattered to various states. He loved his house, neighborhood, spouse, the extra dollars his new job brought. Every turn had more opportunities than negatives. "I learned that a person has to be looking for the opportunities," he continued, "or they tend to pass you by."

Show your people how to view change as opportunity.

Ask the Consultant's Question

The art of continual change includes asking the consultant's question. Consultants do their work by asking, "What needs doing that isn't being done … or could be done better?" You can be your own internal consultant. But don't just ask the question at the beginning or close of each workday. It's a mindset. You ask the question continually as you go about your work.

Mary Westheimer knew publishing inside and out. She had worked as a freelance writer, editor, and book packager. When she was introduced to the Internet in 1994 she was amazed and wide-eyed. She saw potential and lots of things that needed doing. And it all involved publishing. "I saw so much opportunity," she recalls. "I knew it was going to change everything, the way we do business, the way we communicate, the way we make decisions," she adds.

Lots of things that need doing, Westheimer realized, in addition to lots of things that can be done better. And so BookZone.com was born. Now it gets more than 19 million hits a year. It's the largest publishing community with over 3,500 publishers and authors.

What needs doing that isn't being done? Or could be done better?

Edna Roberts had worked in the shipping department for nine years. One day as she was filling out a complex routing form, she stopped. "Why am I doing all of this?" she asked herself, out loud. Edna began looking at the form in a new way. "It's too long, too complicated, and asks too many questions that don't need to be asked," she said. Then she revised it.

Edna reduced completion time by over 50 percent and saved a bundle of dollars for the company. It wasn't long until Edna was asked to review all the forms to see if they could be streamlined. Now she's working on the shipping processes themselves.

At a leading consumer products company, people from different units who work together on special projects got talking about all the meetings they had to attend: Too many, they agreed; wasted too much time; and too many times, they sat in a meeting for an hour when it could have been taken care of in 15 minutes. Something could be done better.

The employees developed a plan to evaluate each meeting beforehand. Key people discussed the agenda prior to each meeting, the amount of time each item warranted based on importance was assigned, and the information distributed to all the people who should attend. In many instances they realized there was no real need for a meeting involving nine people. Two or three people could take care of it, because that's who it involved.

"We cut meeting time by over 50 percent," reports one manager. "That releases us for lots of other things, like meeting our year's goals," she adds.

As a leader, listen to the suggestions and ideas that your people bring to you. Let them lay out what needs doing or could be done better, and their plan to fix it. Take it seriously. Take action to make the changes. Or at least try out these suggestions. Show them their input is important. You will find that your people's involvement enhances the workplace and leads to high performance.

You create continuous change by constantly looking for ways to enhance performance, quality, and service to customers. Asking the consultant's question is one way to get a work group started in creating continuous change.

6. Be Someone Others Enjoy Working With

When organizations go through any kind of change, there are always new people around you. Some are new leaders. Others are new co-workers. Others are just people you see, but you don't interact with them in any way other than to say hello in the break room.

With all the change taking place, make certain you are the kind of person others enjoy working with. And here's how you can define it. Involve your whole work unit in this activity, because the more who get involved, the more impact the action has.

First, have the group brainstorm to make as long a list as possible of the kinds of people they *do not like* working with—you know, people who grumble, don't smile, don't do their share, and so on. Don't worry if someone says they don't like to work with quiet people, and someone else says they do. If someone doesn't like to work with a certain kind of person, list it. When the list seems complete (it never really is), then discuss what's there. What are the commonalities of each item on the list?

Second, have the group make a list of the kinds of people they *do like* working with. Again, make it as complete as possible. When it seems complete, discuss the commonalities.

Third, have each person ask themselves, "*Am I the kind of person that others like working with?*" Then ask them to complete Activity 8-2.

Activity 8-2. Needed Changes

What are the changes I need to make in order to make change work and be the kind of person others like to work with?

____

____

____

____

____

____

____

____

____

____

____

More Skills

Here are even more skills to practice the art of continual change:

- Have a system in place so that new people get acquainted with the workplace and their new co-workers. Remember, your best friends were at one time total strangers.
- Look for ways to do more. If you get done with one assignment, look around for ways to help others, rather than just sit.
- Keep track of the results of your work. Make a list of the things you've done each quarter. For each item, ask yourself, "So what?" Use action words to describe your results.
- Keep a record of innovations in other organizations that you read about or hear others talk about. Ask, "*How might this work in our organization?*" Tell others.

- Find time to relax and recharge. Create a "quiet place" where you can just sit and be. Maybe you read. Maybe you listen to music. Maybe you talk with others. Do whatever it is that helps you recharge and be ready for the next day.

Will There be More Change?

Of course there will. Leading in the tough times of major organizational change will be an expected management skill by the end of this decade.

* * *

"Afraid of asking too much of our people,
we often ask too little of ourselves."

(Richard S. Deems)

Chapter Nine: How Do I Handle Layoffs and Downsizings?

When Todd McDonald downsized American Media, about 20 percent of the workforce was cut. After people had been notified, both remaining and exiting employees were still talking with all of the company's leaders. There were no lawsuits and no bad press. The downsizing got only about an inch of ink on an inside page of the business section, two weeks later.

Contrast that with a downsizing of only 5 managers, out of more than 350 employees, that occurred at a company in the same city a few weeks earlier. It made front-page news, and several articles were published in the week following the downsizing. It even made the 10 o'clock news on two of the city's three local TV stations. And the press wasn't good.

What makes the difference? It's all in how you do it.

Five Reasons to Do It with Care

There are at least five reasons why you need to be concerned about doing a downsizing. Each one of these reasons, and the issues behind them, can do you in. It's all about leadership in tough times.

Litigation. It can cost from $5,000 to $25,000 to merely respond to a letter of intent to sue from a disgruntled worker. So it costs you money. But it also costs you lost reputation.

Effects on remaining employees. If remaining employees feel their exiting friends were treated fairly, then there are few problems. But if remaining employees *perceive* that their friends were not treated fairly, you have several major problems: lowered performance, higher absenteeism, reduced morale, and increased turnover.

Effects on decision makers. Conducting layoffs the right way reduces the stress on key leaders. It enables them to deal with other issues with more energy and less cluttered minds.

Future recruiting status. Job hunters talk among themselves. They talk about the great places to work, and the places to stay away from. Do a downsizing the right way and people will talk about how great a company you lead.

Marketplace reputation. The public pays attention to what they hear about organizations, what they read about in the newspaper, and what they watch on TV. If you doubt that statement, think back to what happened to Arthur Andersen.

For each employee, there are many people involved in a downsizing, and they all talk. How many people? Count them up:

- The employee ___
- The employee's spouse and children (if any) ___
- Family and friends of the employee's spouse ___
- Other relatives of the employee ___
- Co-workers ___
- Other friends within the organization ___
- Friends and social contacts ___
- Neighbors ___
- Family and friends of children's friends ___

That number can come close to 100. With this many people talking about what they think of your organization, make sure you do it right. You want them talking about how great your organization is because of the way you handled the layoffs. Remember: Work as if people mattered.

How Do I Select Who Goes?

Selecting which jobs to eliminate can be relatively simple. You take a look at your business needs and then identify the number and kinds of jobs it will take to turn the plan into actuality. But what do you do if you need only five night supervisors and you have eight, or you need only 15 IT people and you have 21—and all are good performers?

How you select who goes and who stays is a significant effort. Here are some guidelines.

1. Deal with performance issues early.

Good management deals with performance issues as they occur, not when they accumulate. If you have people whose work is not up to standard, then they should already be on some kind of performance improvement process. If that's not where you are, then postpone the downsizing until you've effectively dealt with performance issues.

2. Establish your criteria and apply it to the whole enterprise.

Now that you've taken care of performance issues, you're ready to establish a single criteria for people elimination. In determining this criteria you have choices. You can eliminate people by tenure, by job title or classification, or by a percentage from each department. These are just three ways to make those hard decisions.

What has worked well in other organizations is a criterion for downsizing that includes three factors: tenure, performance, and potential for future performance.

Tenure. Most organizations want to reward employees who've been with them for a time. They've been there through the organization's drive to success. And often they are the ones who can accommodate more change because they've already mastered some of your prior changes.

Performance. Another part of your criteria can be overall job performance. Out of 10 people, there are probably several exemplary performers. But there are also probably several who meet the minimum standards, but nothing more. Performance can be one.

Potential. The third part of the criteria has to do with future potential. Of those within a job classification where cuts will be made, who are the ones with the most potential for what's coming ahead? These are the people you want to keep.

Numeric values. Your leadership team can review the criteria and assign a numeric value to each item. As each person is reviewed, a numeric score is given based on the three criteria (or the number of criteria you identify). From that point on it's a review of numbers.

Apply the criteria consistently throughout the entire organization. Without some kind of objective criteria to evaluate employees, work unit managers are left to make subjective decisions. Subjective decisions can lead to subtle forms of discrimination, which can lead to litigation. Worse yet, it can lead to the workplace reputation that your organization is not a great place to work.

How Can I Test for Fairness?

There is a relatively easy way for you to test for subtle discrimination before the downsizing occurs. You do a statistical analysis of your workforce before the downsizing and after the downsizing, based on the people you've identified who will exit.

Figure 9-1 is an example, based on age.

Figure 9-1. Statistical Analysis by Age

Age Grouping	Before	After
Over 60	8%	7%
50–59	24%	12%
40–49	29%	27%
30–39	29%	34%
20–29	10%	20%

Ooops! The illustration in Figure 9-1 suggests you might have done some subtle discrimination. Going from 8% to 7% in the over 60 group is probably OK. But going from 24% to only 12% in the 50–59 age bracket suggests that you've targeted, intentionally or not, people in their 50s. It would be difficult to defend your actions should all those over 50 decide to pursue litigation. And it would be easy for them to say you got rid of the 50-somethings just so that you could keep the 20-somethings.

You can do the same kind of analysis for sex, ethnic origin, educational level, years with the organization, salary levels, and whatever else you might want to consider. We'd at least recommend you do an analysis for age, sex, and ethnic origin.

The before and after numbers are information you can share with remaining employees, exiting employees, and even the media. If your percentages remain close, it will help all employees understand that you did not seek out one particular group of employees to exit. It will help morale. And you can count on it being talked about in the marketplace. Being fair and sharing the numbers might be one of the most important recruiting tools you have for the future.

How Do I Tell the People Who Will Exit?

A bank manager walked into her office one morning and found an envelope on her desk with her name written on it. She opened it and read, "Dear Terminated Employee."

This is not the way to do it. If you want to be able to recruit the best people in the near future, then you must implement carefully selected processes. Here are the top issues that must be considered.

1. Use care and control.

Part of your job in telling people their jobs have been eliminated is to do it in such a way that you show the company truly cares about people. Caring about people goes beyond that slogan on your wall. It shows itself in actions. So you take time to do it right. And do it with as much finesse as you can.

At the same time you stay in control of the process. A downsizing is a very emotional thing for most people. If you're not careful, you can lose control, not only of the downsizing process, but of your entire workplace. If you tell people in ways that anger remaining employees, you've lost control, and it might take you weeks to fully regain it.

2. The manager/executive conducts the meeting.

If the downsizing involves just a few people, then perhaps the CEO and each person's manager can inform each exiting employee. If it's a larger downsizing, however, the kind of scheduling it would take for individual notification might take too long.

The basic guideline is the exiting employee's direct manager or executive tells the exiting employee. If employees are told individually (see below), then two people need to be present during the meeting. Both should be either supervisors or managers.

3. You can tell them individually or through small groups or sometimes even a large group.

Which is best? It's a tough question, and there is no easy answer. Just remember, however, care and control. If it is a small number of people who are involved, you may find it works better to tell each person individually.

Can you inform one person and then move on to the next person and have it all completed within an hour? Or two hours? As a general rule, if it takes longer than two hours to inform people through individual meetings you will want to consider group meetings. Otherwise, the disruption grows each time someone goes into a meeting. Fifteen minutes after you've begun your downsizing, the entire workforce will be waiting and watching to see who "goes into the room" next.

If your downsizing involves a good number of people from different departments, you will want to think through the advantages of telling them in small groups, by departments, or one large group.

You explain the assistance to be provided, how and when people should retrieve their personal belongings, talk about references, answer any questions, and introduce them to the job transition specialists who you've asked to be on-site.

4. Do the same things in all your locations.

Many organizations have more than one location, even within the same city. So how do you handle a downsizing with multiple locations? Maybe even in different time zones?

You plan it so that people get told the same way in each location and at about the same time. Why? If you have more than one location, you can count on the other locations hearing about what's going on within minutes of the first termination. The rumor system runs swiftly and deeply.

5. Tell the people early in the week and early in the day.

Friday afternoon is the worst time to do a downsizing, despite what others will try to tell you. First, people have no opportunity to begin the adjustment before the first weekend as "unemployed" comes around. For some reason, the first weekend is the toughest.

Second, remaining employees will talk. If you terminate on Friday afternoon, many exiting and remaining employees will be talking on the phone over the weekend. They'll be talking about how bad a deal people got. How it isn't fair that one person lost their job while someone else didn't. Come Monday morning, you might have an angry workforce. And you've had no opportunity before the weekend to answer questions or tell people about the assistance being provided to those who exited.

Third, when you terminate early in the week and early in the day, you have opportunity to observe reactions from remaining employees. If some people have questions, you can answer them before the end of the day. If some remaining employees are angry, you have opportunity to deal with it before those people have an opportunity to let it grow. In other words, you stay in control.

We recommend announcing the downsizing early in the week and early in the day. We prefer Tuesday mornings. That gives you Monday to make one last assessment of your plans, of the workplace, and of your scripts of what you'll say. When you leave the office Monday afternoon, you leave knowing your task for the next day. You can plan on spending the rest of the week with your remaining people, assuring them that things are going to get better.

Why are Friday firings so popular? Some people say it's easier for those exiting. But that's not the case. It's easiest for the managers and decision-makers who can make the announcement and then not have to deal with any of the fallout. Friday firings are for wimps.

6. Plan, prepare, and practice what to say.

Downsizings are not the time to go with the flow and say whatever comes to mind. Do that and you could end up in court. Worse yet, you could say things that shove your organization to the bottom of the list of great places to work.

Here are five major guidelines.

First, this is not the time for chitchat. When you meet the person (or persons) whom you are about to inform of their job elimination, don't take time for chitchat. Don't bother to talk about the weather, or the latest sports news, or how the kids are. Greet the person cordially, but get to the reason for the meeting.

Second, state the reason for the meeting. Get right to the point. Tell them why you're meeting. Briefly explain why the downsizing is necessary. And begin describing the kinds of assistance the person will receive.

Third, don't argue. This is not the time to get involved in a detailed discussion as to why the downsizing is occurring, or even why this person's position has been eliminated. Be ready to state, sometimes again and again, "John, I'm not here to argue with you. The decision has been made, and you and I aren't going to change it here. Let's move on and let me tell you about the assistance that will be provided for you and the others…."

If you get into an argument, you lose.

Fourth, prepare your script. Take time to write out what you will say. Anticipate the questions you might be asked. Write out what your answers will be. Make the script self-serving for you and the organization. Review your script to be sure you show care, and maintain control by saying nothing that might hurt the organization in the future.

If the downsizing is large, you might want to work with other managers to develop a single script that works best for your organization. Downsizings that have resulted in the most disruption have consistently been those where managers have said, "Oh, I can wing it—I don't need a script." Insert the BS phrase here.

Fifth, practice what you're going to say. Going through in your head what you plan on saying, and actually hearing yourself say the words out loud, are two different experiences. Practice, out loud, what you intend to say. The most successful downsizings we've coordinated included training managers in the entire process. We've shown managers what to say, made them practice, and then provided them feedback. Everybody has a chance to hear themselves say out loud, "Jane, our meeting is to inform you that your position has been eliminated… and to describe the kinds of assistance ABC Organization will provide you during this transition."

But don't say anything that even comes close to…

- "Well, John, I don't agree either, but this is what I've been told to do…"
- "Yeah, I know John, this seems like a bum deal…"
- "Well, John, I don't know why you're included, maybe it's because you're over 50…"
- "Yeah, John, I know there's a lot of work to get done, maybe they'll hire new people…"
- "Yeah, it seems like the top floor just can't make any good decisions these days…"

Practice what you'll say. It keeps you from doing dumb things.

Figure 9-2 shows a plausible scenario for telling an individual that her position has been eliminated in the downsizing.

Figure 9-2. Individual Meeting

Manager:	Thanks, Carmen, for stopping what you've been doing and coming to this meeting. I think you know Lori who manages the marketing unit. Please be seated Carmen and let's get on with our meeting.
Employee:	I've heard rumors there's going to be a downsizing. That's what this is about isn't it…
Manager:	Well, Carmen, as you know, the international market has slowed and our sales have been cut by more than 35 percent. The company's leaders and board of directors have struggled with what to do and finally reached the decision to eliminate 25 positions. Carmen, our meeting today is to inform you that your position has been eliminated…. And your employment with ABC Org ends very soon….
Employee:	What? You're eliminating my job? After all that I've done?

Figure 9-2 (continued)

Manager:	The decision as to what jobs to eliminate wasn't easy. The organization looked at the business plan, identified the resources it would take to bring that plan to reality, and then made the hard decisions as to what expenses and jobs to cut.
Employee:	Yeah, well, some kind of reward I get for doing good work.
Manager:	Yes, Carmen, you have done good work. It's not been an easy decision to make. But rather than focus on a decision that's been made, let me explain the assistance you'll receive to help you find a new job where you can thrive....
Employee:	But ...
Manager:	Carmen, here's a letter that summarizes the assistance you'll be receiving. Let's go through that letter together.... (See Figure 9-4 for sample letter.) Well, Carmen, do you have any questions?
Employee:	Yeah, when am I done? When can I get my things? The more I think about this, the more I think it's a bum deal. I want to talk with the president. She'll see that I'm the wrong person to go.
Manager:	Yes, Hilga will be glad to talk with you. She was part of the decision-making process. When we're done with our meeting, let's check with her office and see when she might be available.
	(Manager answers questions)
Manager:	Thank you, Carmen, for understanding ABC Org's situation. You can count on me to provide a reference for you. We want to keep in touch with you, and we want to know where you find a new position. Now, let me introduce you to your transition coach who will help you in your search to find a new position....
Employee:	Thanks, you've been helpful. I really don't need to see Hilga. But thanks for being willing to set it up. Now, who are these people who will help me find a new job?

Does it go as smoothly as in Figure 9-2? Sometimes.

And sometimes it doesn't. But if you don't plan and practice and anticipate, it will never go smoothly. Just remember the guidelines above. Anticipate how each person may react. And prepare for each possible question that may get asked. The key is preparation.

Your script when talking with a group will be slightly different. Figure 9-3 shows a sample script for a group.

Figure 9-3. Sample Script

Thank you for coming to this meeting. I'm sure you're all wondering what it's about, so let me get right to the purpose of our meeting. As you're aware, ABC Org has been going through some loss of market and downturn of profits. We've looked hard at our business plan, made a number of corrective steps, and regret that we have to do one more thing.

Our meeting today is to inform you that we are eliminating 49 positions today. Your positions are the ones being eliminated. You are not the only ones whose positions are being eliminated. Earlier today we told Kay, VP of Investments, and Sam, VP of Marketing, that their positions have been eliminated and their responsibilities divided among the remaining officers.

What I'd like to do in our time together is to describe the various kinds of assistance we'll provide for each of you, answer any questions, and introduce you to the people who will help you find new jobs.

(Review the assistance, hand out the individual packets—see below.)

(Answer questions.)

You will have options in getting your personal belongings. (Explain the options.)

I'll be around the rest of today and the rest of this week. If you have any questions or would like to talk directly with me, stop by. Now, let me introduce the people who can help you find new positions where you can be successful….

Write your own script. Anticipate the questions. Prepare your answers beforehand. Practice. Practice. Practice. And for several days before the announcements, eat less, drink less, exercise more, and get more sleep than usual. At the end of the big day, find some special way to relax. Maybe a dinner out with spouse or special friends. Or a hike. Or racquetball. Or sit in the spa. Be good to yourself.

7. Have the letter ready.

Over the years we've learned that this letter can save you lots of time. It also helps people who are exiting, since their initial reaction is often shock and they have a tendency to forget details after being told their job has been cut. The letter, however, gives them something tangible to look at when they get home. They won't need to call you. Instead, they can look at their letter. A sample letter is shown in Figure 9-4. When you have this kind of an individualized letter ready to hand out during the notification meeting, you save time for everyone. It shows you care. And it keeps you in control.

8. Provide time for people to get their things.

Back in the '90s we often recommended that people come back in an evening or the next weekend to retrieve their personal belongings. For upper level managers that still might be preferred.

Otherwise, today we recommend that you give people an option. Either they can get their things now, say their good-byes, and leave the building. Or, they can come back some evening or even on Saturday morning. What's important is that the exiting people have a choice in how they bring closure.

For those who want to stay for a while and talk with friends, give them the opportunity. Sure, it will cost you in terms of lost productivity. But in the long term you'll gain. People will say, "Gee, we work for an organization that cares."

That will make a great difference two years from now when you're recruiting again.

9. Make arrangements for people to get home.

Some of your people probably car pool. Or have neighbors or spouses drop them off and pick them up. Or rely on public transportation. For those people, make arrangements to get them home as soon as they are ready to leave. Having them stay the rest of the day, however, is not an option.

Figure 9-4. Sample Letter

Dear (Name)

This letter is to confirm our meeting of (date) and to summarize the assistance you will receive. Because of a downsizing, your position was one of several to be eliminated.

To assist you in this transition ABC Org will provide...

- X weeks of severance (salary continuation) based on the company policy of two weeks salary continuance for each year or part of a year of employment.
- A corresponding number of weeks of health coverage. After X weeks, you will be able to continue your healthcare benefits by paying the full premium. More information will be sent in the near future.
- Letters of reference will be prepared as you need them. Please contact me directly when you need such a letter.
- Job transition assistance will be provided by (name of company) and they will begin their work with you today. These people are hired by ABC Org to assist you in finding a new position. They will coach you in how to prepare a resume, how to find job openings, how to effectively interview, and how to maintain your energy for a successful job search.

In addition, you will receive compensation for X weeks of vacation accrued, but not taken, according to our company policy.

Your contribution to ABC Org is appreciated, and we want to provide all the assistance we can during this transition. If you have questions, please call me directly at (phone number).

Sincerely,

Manager
Phone Number

10. Plan on total disruption the day people are told.

It isn't going to be easy the day of the downsizing. There will be confusion, anger, frustration, and lots of unhappy people. And not a great deal will get done.

Take a look at what absolutely has to get accomplished on downsizing day and look at the people you can count on. As the downsizing meetings begin to take place, pull those people aside. Tell them what's taking place. Tell them what absolutely needs to get done by the end of the day. Ask—don't demand—for their help in getting it done.

Otherwise, the day is going to be like few others.

11. Use common sense.

Cancel all executive/leadership trips and vacations until at least two weeks after the downsizing. Maybe even three or four weeks. If Senior VP Melissa takes off for the Bahamas two days after the downsizing, it won't set well with employees. If VP Harry takes off for a professional development meeting in Las Vegas the day after the downsizing, there will be employees wondering why the organization has dollars to send that jerk to Vegas to play.

And don't show up the next day in your new BMW.

12. Prepare a summary of the meeting and file it.

It's important to summarize each notification meeting. This summary doesn't need to be long, but it needs to reflect what was said, who said what, and what took place. A sample summary is shown in Figure 9-5.

Figure 9-5. Sample Meeting Summary

On Tuesday, May 15, 2001, Sharon Brownfield and I met with Tom Ormandy to tell him of his position elimination. Ormandy was very angry at first, and we did not argue, but rather listened to him. Sharon continued to lead him back to the topic of transition assistance and gave him his letter. He asked several questions about who would be doing his work and the length of his severance. We introduced him to the transition specialists and Ormandy shook hands with both of us and thanked us for our encouragement.

Both people managing the meeting sign and date the report and it goes into the downsizing file. Will you ever need these reports? Seldom. But it helps in case you do. It's worth the time to make your report, sign it, and file it.

13. Start at the top.

When there are multiple levels of employees who will be exiting, begin at the top. The higher-level people get told first. If a Senior VP's position is being eliminated, do that one first. Then the other VPs, Directors, and Managers.

Then you can notify the other employees.

Why? Because it shows that the downsizing doesn't just hit the little guys. It hits the top ones, too. Because some top people are involved, it makes it easier for the majority of employees to support the downsizing—or at least to understand it.

How Do I Tell the People Who Will Remain?

Of all the downsizings in which we've participated, one of the very first set the standard for telling remaining employees. You tell them direct, in person, and as quickly as possible.

In an insurance company of about 750 employees, the downsizing was conducted in one day. People whose jobs were eliminated were told in meetings outside of their work area, by departments. As soon as everyone was told in one department the team moved on to the next. It worked in that culture.

After everyone had been told, CEO Jim Luhrs returned to each department. He brought with him people to answer department phones and he gathered the employees around him. He stood in the middle and briefly told the people what had happened, the kind of assistance exiting employees would receive, and the severance policy that was in place. Then he asked for questions.

"I took a lot of heat," Jim recalls, "and some people swore at me and there was lots of anger. But the next morning," he adds, "people started dropping by my office at 7 a.m. to thank me for telling them in person and not in a memo." Bottom-line? "It was worth all the gaff I took, and it got us back to normal more quickly than had I hid in my office for the day!"

Remember Jim and his story as you plan how to tell remaining employees.

Here are five guidelines for informing remaining employees.

1. *Tell them quickly.* As soon as everyone whose job is being eliminated in a department or unit or location has been told, then tell the remaining employees. Or conduct the meetings simultaneously. Tell them directly and in person. Tell them that the organization didn't want to do it, but it had to. Tell them there was a downsizing affecting *X* number of people. Tell them briefly why. And outline the transition assistance those exiting people will receive.

2. *Tell them in person.* The message should be given in person, not through some memo or posting on the bulletin board or even an e-mail. E-mails might be an effective communication tool, but the subject of people losing their jobs is too important for such an impersonal means of sharing information.

3. *The top brass talks.* Who goes around and tells remaining employees what has happened? The highest-level people you can get! This means the top level are involved in going around to the units and explaining what has happened. If the CEO can't do it, then go to the executive in charge of that department. Let that person visit the unit and explain what happened, tell them why the downsizing occurred, and talk about all the kinds of assistance people will be given to help them find a new position. Our own personal bias is that the CEO needs to be directly involved in telling remaining employees. It sends a vital message to the workplace.

4. *Coach the people in what to say.* People who talk with remaining employees need to practice what they will say. They need a great script. And they need to hear themselves say the words, out loud, *before* they begin this task. You dare not excuse yourself from preparing. Be ready for questions. Answer them directly and honestly. A sample script is shown in Figure 9-6.

5. *Make yourself easily available.* The day of the downsizing, and the several days afterward, is not the time to take off. Sure, you might be tired and you might want to get away from it all. Being a leader in tough times means sticking it out. If the others have to stay, so do you.

Figure 9-6. Sample Script

> *Folks, I want to personally tell you that this morning we downsized our work force by X number of people. This is a task we didn't want to do. However, as the leadership group analyzed our business plan, we realized we needed to reduce costs. One of the ways we chose to do this is through the downsizing. There are other cost-cutting efforts that will be in place also, which include...*
>
> *We want to do as much as we can to help these people find new, satisfying jobs, as quickly as possible. According to our policy, people will receive severance, which is salary continuation, based on their length of employment, with a minimum of X weeks and maximum of X weeks. In addition, people will continue their healthcare coverage for X months, at which time they can continue it on their own if they choose.*
>
> *We're also providing job transition assistance, and (company) will start working with these people tomorrow morning on how to identify their best skills, how to write a resume, how to find job openings, how to ace an interview, and how to keep up a person's energy. Our department managers will also be calling department managers in other organizations in our community to tell them of the availability of these people.*
>
> *That kind of summarizes what we did and why and how we're helping these people. I'm ready to try to answer whatever questions you have....*

The best strategy is to make yourself even more available than usual. Walk around the workplace. Be visible. Take time to talk with people. If someone asks you a question about the downsizing or the company's future, take time to respond—openly. And let others gather around you if they want to listen, too.

Is Career Transition Assistance Really Necessary?

In one word, yes! It shows you care. It shows you care even about the people who are leaving. And if you care about the people who are leaving, you must really care about the people who stay. It's the ultimate in showing that you're an organization in it for the long haul. And you appreciate all the people who've had a hand in your success.

There are basically three kinds of service: individual, one-on-one sessions; group sessions; or a combination of group and individual sessions. Several years ago, we developed a combination of group and individual sessions. At first it was a way to provide assistance for organizations that didn't think they could afford the individual service. What we've found over the years is that the combination works very well.

We've provided career transition assistance for more than 20 years. We've pioneered several of today's best practices. And we believe that in whatever format you provide assistance, it needs to cover these content areas:

- Dealing with job loss, using the Deems Job Loss Reaction Cycle
- Identifying what you do best and your top job options
- Developing a results-oriented resume (not from some computer program)
- How to find and respond to job openings
- How to research the job and the organization
- Interviewing strategies and practice
- How to negotiate the final offer
- Maintaining energy to turn job hunting into JobGetting

The mood needs to be upbeat, positive, and encouraging—no sniveling.

If you can't afford one-on-one service (at least 15–25 hours of assistance over a period of several months), then go for the combination. It will take two to four half-day sessions to cover the material, and two individual sessions to provide the most cost-effective assistance. Research shows that the quick, band-aid approach that is more talk than substance is not effective.

Why go to the expense of providing career transition assistance? Because it shows you care. It shows remaining people that if something happens to their jobs, they'll receive assistance in finding a new job, too. It shows the marketplace that you're a company that truly cares about its people. Even the people who have to exit.

Figure 9-7. Downsizing Checklist

Checklist

Have we...

- ❑ Reviewed the business plan?
- ❑ Identified other ways to reduce costs in addition to eliminating positions?
- ❑ Identified the human resources we need in order to reach our business plan goals and objectives?
- ❑ Identified the kinds and numbers of positions that should be eliminated?
- ❑ Established a criteria for deciding whose positions will be eliminated?
- ❑ Followed the criteria consistently throughout the entire organization?
- ❑ Identified the people whose jobs will be eliminated?
- ❑ Conducted a detailed analysis of our workplace both before and after the proposed downsizing by age, sex, ethnic origin, years of service, and any other categories?
- ❑ Found any inconsistencies and taken corrective actions?
- ❑ Reviewed existing severance policy and made any changes to enhance the assistance people will receive?
- ❑ Decided what works best in our workplace: tell everyone in small groups, individually, or in one large group?
- ❑ Designated one person to deal with the media and informed all managers to refer media calls to that single person?
- ❑ Provided media training for the designated media contact?

Figure 9-7 (continued)

- ❑ Set a date for announcing the downsizing and cleared calendars of all people involved?
- ❑ Trained people who will be conducting the meetings on how to conduct a downsizing notification meeting.
- ❑ Arranged to have individual letters prepared to distribute at the notification meeting(s)?
- ❑ Scheduled the rooms needed to conduct the downsizing notification meetings?
- ❑ Selected a job transition organization to provide transition assistance?
- ❑ Scheduled the transition services organization so that they can be on-site and begin their work the next day?
- ❑ Coached everyone involved in notifying employees of the downsizing in how to physically and mentally prepare, i.e., extra sleep, extra exercise, and reduced food and alcohol intake?
- ❑ Reviewed this list in detail and honestly answered each question?

If you're called upon to lead in the tough times of a downsizing, then do it with care and control. And do it with class.

* * *

"Worry is misuse of the imagination."

(Anonymous)

Chapter Ten: What If I'm Asked to Do Something Illegal?

The collapse of several major corporations, like Enron, WorldCom, Tyco, ImClone, Global Crossing, and Arthur Andersen, all appear to have had one thing in common. Leaders were asking people to do things that weren't legal. The newspaper and TV reports have given lots of space to some of the illegal operations taking place.

Somebody had to think up those various schemes. Somebody had to ask others to do the tasks.

And all too often, it appears, somebody said, "Hey, I didn't do it, that other person did." So what do you do if your boss asks you to do something that isn't legal? Or hints at it? Or your boss doesn't ask, but demands?

You don't think it's right.

And yet, you're afraid that if you don't do it, you might get fired—or demoted, or red-lined, or worse. "Illegal things get done because unscrupulous leaders know that someone will do them," states Washington, D.C., attorney Charles D. Goldman. "The employee needs the paycheck, and the leader knows it. So the leader asks. Too often, the employee does," Goldman adds.

Here are the actions you can take if you think you're being asked to do something illegal.

Is It Illegal or Unethical?

Your first action is to determine if what you're being asked to do is merely against your ethics—your values—or whether it is actually illegal. If it's against your values, you may take a look at the whole situation and count the cost of declining. If what you're being asked to do is so flagrantly contrary to your values, you may want to decline.

If you decline to do the activity because it's against your value system, be ready to explain why. Share your reasons. Make them clear and to the point. To say, "No I can't do that, it's against my values" is not an adequate statement. Say, "I find this request to be very difficult because it asks me to do something that is contrary to my values. Let me explain how and why...." You fill in the empty space. Your rationale will be important to the leader who has asked you to do the questionable task.

The best rationale, reports Goldman, is to say: "Sorry, I won't do this. I'm a loyal employee of this organization. I want to do what's in this company's best interest, and I don't think this is in the company's best interest." If you think the action might be illegal, ask if your boss is aware that what she or he is asking you to do might be illegal. Maybe your boss isn't aware that the action is against the law. Or maybe your boss doesn't care. If your boss is aware of the illegality, ask your boss to explain why this is something that has to be done.

If the person continues to insist you do the task, or if you believe the task is illegal, then ask for further clarification.

Ask for Insight from Specialists

If you believe the request is truly illegal, like shredding documents that have been subpoenaed, then step back and ask for clarification from specialists at the upper levels. Ask for review from the organization's chief counsel, or chief auditor. Ask counsel to review the action to see if it's contrary to laws and/or guidelines. Ask to see if the counsel says it's OK, or if the counsel wants more information.

Your request can be simply stated: "I think this is something that might not be legal, and I'd be more comfortable if we sought out a specialist's advice. You know, someone like our chief counsel."

Congress in 2002 passed new laws dealing with accountability of boards of directors and financial reporting. Auditors are now required to report questionable and illegal bookkeeping practices of corporations. And it appears that corporate attorneys may be faced with the same requirements.

In an Associated Press report of August 13, 2002, SEC Chair Harvey Pitt is quoted as telling the American Bar Association that "Lawyers for public companies represent the company as a whole and its shareholder-owners, not the managers who hire and fire them. In addition to auditors and corporate leaders," Pitt states, "Congress believes that lawyers representing public companies also have responsibilities requiring governmental definition." This means that if a corporate lawyer knows of illegal practices, it is the law that lawyers report the illegal activity.

Taking the request to higher counsel puts the responsibility for determining the legality of the action on those who must ultimately sign off on the organization's activities. If counsel says it's all right to fulfill the request, then you probably need to carry out the action. If counsel says "I'm not sure," then it is up to counsel to make the determination. And you're off the hook.

Remember to use phrases like "I'm trying to do what's in the company's best interests." Or "As a loyal employee, I don't want to do anything that will get the company in trouble or break the law in any way."

What if your boss refuses to go to counsel? Then you go to counsel, advises Goldman, and report back to your boss what counsel said in writing.

Ask for It in Writing

Ask to have the request put in writing so that your boss has a copy and you have a copy that you keep with you. Make sure the memo is dated and signed, preferably by both. Putting it in writing says, "OK, I don't think it's right, so when you tell me I have to do it, and I do it, then it becomes your responsibility."

Sometimes bosses make comments, but they're really demands. If your boss says, "Gee, I sure wish these documents didn't exist—it would make it so much easier on everybody," then don't do anything. Sure, your boss might be suggesting that you go shred the documents. You could get rid of them and make your boss happy.

But if you did the act, you go to jail, while your boss reports to authorities, "Hey, I just made an observation. I didn't intend that the employee shred the files." And your boss heads home for dinner.

Tell Others

If you're still getting pressured to do something you know is illegal, then draft a memo and send it to at least three other persons you know. Two of those should be from the same company. Explain what you are being asked to do and why. Include why you think it isn't right. Refer to reports and reactions from counsel. Make it in enough detail so that the people will understand what you are being asked to do and why. Date, sign, send, and file the memo.

You can also send this memo to another leader within the organization or even a member of the board of directors. There are many instances of leadership changes taking place because some employee stepped up and informed the board of directors. In many instances, boards only know what the C-level (CEO, CFO, CIO, etc.) people tell them. Reports from other employees are often viewed with appreciation.

Don't Do It

When push comes to shove, don't do the illegal act. Quietly explain to your boss why his or her demand is illegal and/or unethical. Quietly explain that it is against your values and principles of real leadership. Quietly explain that the requested action is illegal. Quietly explain that you have conferred with others about the illegality of the request. Report your findings that others concur it is neither legal, right, or fair. Be ready for the consequences.

"You can get fired," Goldman admits, "but at least you won't be in jail."

"But It's Just Good Business Practice"

That's what you hear sometimes: You have to stretch the truth once in a while just to get the account or keep it. Back in the dot-com frenzy, one of the most commonly used tactics was to sell advertising space that didn't exist. Salespeople would tell their clients that it was a 1-in-300,000 chance that they'd actually see their banner ad on the Internet, but it was there.

People were pushed to meet their sales quotas. They'd do anything they could to meet the numbers. The July 2002 issue of *Sales & Marketing Management* includes an investigative report on corporate deceitful practices. What they found was in many organizations, the rule was to "Do whatever it took to close those (big) deals." Promises get made that can never be kept.

It happened in the insurance industry, too. A number of years ago there were many insurance salespeople who were encouraged to stretch things a bit—make projections about investments that just weren't true and that weren't going to happen. Big names and small names in life insurance got caught. Most paid for it in reputation, lost business, fines, and ruined careers.

But as one insurance executive said, "Hey, we were all doing it, so what's the big deal?"

The big deal was that it was dishonest. And there are many policy holders today who did not, and will not, reap the benefits they were "guaranteed."

For an increasing number of salespeople, the deceit isn't worth it. *Sales & Marketing Management* Senior Editor Erin Stout finds that an increasing number of organizations are turning away from commission-based sales. Instead, they are looking for people whose skills are in building and maintaining long-term relationships. Of course, that has been the primary growth strategy promoted by management specialists for decades. And it's honest.

Are these easy actions to take? No. Refusing to take part in an illegal or unethical action may be one of the toughest decisions you'll ever have to make. But you'll sleep better. You'll stay out of jail. And you'll have confidence in knowing that your actions did not contribute to the moral decay of corporate America.

Disclaimer. Since every situation is different, the advice here is not to be construed as legal advice. For further clarification, consult your own attorney or your company's attorney. The information provided is intended as a general guideline only, for people who have been asked to do something that might be determined to be illegal or the employee finds unethical.

* * *

"Today, in all but a rapidly dwindling number of still traditional societies, men and women become leaders by what they do."

(Harland Cleveland)

Chapter Eleven: What Can I Do When the Company's in Financial Trouble?

Since 9/11, the economy has slid downward—a lot. Even before 9/11, the economy had started to nose dive. Repercussions of that day fueled the economic downturn. At WorkLife Design, we had heard various leaders report that orders were declining and growth was slowing since about 1998.

"Growth was only 9 percent instead of 15 percent," some managers reported. As 2000 approached, some managers were telling us, "Orders have dropped well below what they had been five years ago." Companies began wondering how to cut their losses. Some executives decided to lie. For those who insisted that honesty drives their business, it wasn't long before the slide started to show. The growth finally stopped, and the decline set in. Instead of marginal profits, there were noticeable losses.

So what do you do when the company is about to go under? We surveyed turnaround specialists to see what they suggested. Though each had their own special way to attack the situation, there were some commonalities. These include:

1. Acknowledge the problem
2. Open the books
3. Go out of the box
4. Create a shared vision
5. Work as a team
6. Share the glory
7. Don't rest on your laurels

Here's what's involved in each action.

Acknowledge the Problem

The first step is to acknowledge that there is a problem. Take a hard look at what's happening and admit that some things, many things, need to change. "Turnaround is a mentality," states turnaround specialist Pete Taggart. "You have to first admit that there's a problem, and you have to have the mentality that it's not just fine tuning, but it's literally turning things around."

Too many leaders think it's just a matter of fixing one or two things, like coming up with a new marketing plan, or adding a new salesperson, or maybe cutting employee perks in order to pay vendors. "People who survive a downturn," Taggart believes, "are those who feel the water on their feet and say, 'Hey, there's something drastically wrong here, and I better get off this boat.' Those who don't survive are those who say, 'Hey, nothing to worry about, somebody will take care of it.'"

"Denial is very comforting right up until the point you go under," states American Bookstore Association president Neal Conerly. Once you've acknowledged there is a problem, you can do something about it.

How do you know if there's a problem? Stop and take a look at three things.

First, have costs begun to exceed revenue? If so, you have a problem. It may be only a short-term experience. Or it may signal a major issue for you. Don't try to do aggressive, creative accounting. It doesn't work. It's very simple: you add up the numbers and when those numbers given to you are accurate, you can tell if costs exceed revenue.

Part of your research needs to focus on hidden costs—things that are costing you money, but maybe you didn't know about. "You have to have the kinds of accounting and reporting processes that give you the information you need," adds Taggart. For example, at WorkLife Design, a large insurance broker asked us to complete an organizational audit for them. "We've lost three or four of our good IT people," they told us. What we found was that turnover in the broker's IT department the previous six months was more like 57 percent.

We projected it was costing them nearly $1 million a year to recruit, interview, hire, train, and bring new IT people up to speed. But those figures never got to the key decision makers. Here was a cost that got buried. As a leader, you need to ask the kinds of questions that uncover hidden costs: direct questions, hard questions, digging questions. And then see how much trouble you're in.

Second, what's happening to the customer base? Are your 20/80 customers (the 20 percent of your customers who comprise 80 percent of your business) still with you? If they have left you, you might be in serious trouble. "You can't grow a business, let alone maintain it, if your core customers are leaving you," says sales training guru Paul Schnabel.

And, what do you know about your non-customers? If you have 10 percent of the market, there are 90 percent of the people/organizations who aren't using you. Getting to know your non-customers is not easy. But it is the only way to expand your knowledge and your business. And it might be the only way to fix what's broken.

Third, are your best people still with you? When you look around and realize that two or three of your best people have left the organization in the past several months, you need to stop and find out why. Often, it's because they see what's coming, but they haven't seen anyone start to do something about it. So they bail, when they can.

"I've seen this several times," reports insurance executive Tom Van Fossen. "Employees know what's going on when it comes to profits and viability," Van Fossen adds. "If they see a problem, but realize no one is going to do anything about it, they move on while they can move out of strength."

If costs exceed revenue, if your customer base is leaving you, and it's harder to find those really good employees who will stay, you have a problem. Leading in tough times means you acknowledge the reality of problems.

Open the Books

There are a lot of highly successful companies in the world who attribute their success to the open book management (OBM) policy. One of the most widely known is the Brazilian company, Semco. For years, employees have known all the numbers. The company's books—costs, revenues, salaries, and profits—are open to all the employees. "If employees don't know how the company makes money," writes J. Case, "how can they be expected to make the firm more successful?"

Particularly during tough times, employees need to know what's going on. Otherwise, they can't make rational decisions about whether or not to support cuts in jobs, perks, wage increases, or promotions. Not knowing the facts, they will often withhold support for the suggested changes needed to turn the company around.

A privately held manufacturer got itself in financial difficulty. It got to the point that suppliers would deliver only when paid in cash at the plant's doors. Some vendors waited months for full payment. But while the employees were trying hard to make do with worn and outdated manufacturing tools, the owner/CEO purchased a new plane. No, it wasn't a jet. But the cost of the new pressurized six-seater could have gone a long way toward paying down bills, adding new equipment, or providing bonuses.

The owner held all the financial details very tightly. He and the external accountant were the only ones who really knew what was going on. The result: Employees at all levels didn't trust the owner. They had a scrap rate of over 50 percent, absenteeism higher than 20 percent, and turnover more than 35 percent. There was no trust between the workers and the owner.

If you want the support of employees, you need to open the books. Tell them exactly what's going on: what costs are; how much is being lost each week, each month, each year; where surpluses are going; who gets paid what; what the leadership perks are.

When banker Les Olson took over a troubled bank, the first thing he did was to cut costs: no new office equipment, turn off lights, no salary increases. "It has to start at the top," Olson said. So he eliminated his first class plane travel, and flew coach on all trips. He canceled his country club membership. "If I'm not willing to make sacrifices," Olson said, "then I can't ask my people to make sacrifices." In less than two years, the bank was again showing profits.

"You have to set the tone by example," reminds retail manager Mike Gold. "You can't think you're above your people."

What if the information you share puts top leadership, or the owners, in a bad light? Then maybe that's the reason the company is in trouble—too many perks for owners and top managers, not enough paid to people who get the work done. That's the risk of sharing the numbers. Our own belief is that a great disparity between owners and workers is a major problem in and of itself and is probably a primary reason a company finds itself in trouble.

You may need to hold some business literacy workshops so that all employees understand how businesses make money. If employees understand the information contained in financial reports and P/L statements, then they more clearly understand how profits are gleaned. And that leads to employees making decisions about their work that are best for the organization, not just themselves.

What do you share?

- Revenue sources, totals, cash flow trends
- Expenses for raw materials, building, salaries, insurances, and everything
- Salaries of top leaders, and number of people earning various salaries
- Investments of the organization, where and how much
- Surpluses of the organization, where and how much
- Debt of the organization, where and how much
- Monies paid out to consultants, auditors, and other specialists
- And your people will no doubt think of other information they'd like

A word of caution: Before opening the books, bring in a specialist to help you assess the business savvy of your employees. An organizational assessment can identify what else your people need to know about business so that they can understand the books. The assessment can also show you the best ways to begin sharing the numbers. Remember, once you've opened the books it may be difficult to ever close them. But most organizations that have opened their books have no desire to ever close them again.

Go Out of the Box

It's a trite phrase, but we all know what it means. So let's use it. Getting out of the box means thinking in new ways—attacking problems from different perspectives, not just relying on the usual problem-solving actions, and never saying, "But we've never done it this way before." As Taggart reminds us, "You can't turn around an organization by doing what you've been doing. You have to start doing new and different things."

There had never been an ice-cream company like Ben & Jerry's before, until childhood friends Ben Cohen and Jerry Greenfield began working together. But everybody has heard of Ben & Jerry's. They're known for high quality ice cream and frozen yogurt in lots of crazy flavors—out-of-the-box thinking.

There had never been a company like Bertch Cabinet Manufacturing before, either. Founder Gary Bertch realized that after so many people got working in one space, quality and performance declined. The magic number seemed to be around 200. Now Bertch Cabinet Manufacturing has several buildings on its campus, each with about 200 employees. A sense of family, pride in workmanship, and continual innovation are terms descriptive of the workplace culture at Bertch.

"Turning things around," adds Taggart, "means doing things you hadn't thought about six months ago. You get out of the box, and look at your business in new ways." And you don't stop at the first brick wall you hit.

Peter Drucker tells the story of John Wesley Hyatt who had invented the roller bearing. He decided it was just right for the railroad industry. Ball bearings could replace the oily rags used on the axles of freight cars. But the railroads weren't ready for this kind of radical change. After all, they had been stuffing the wheels of their cars with rags soaked in oil to handle the friction for a long time. They liked their rags. The rags worked.

Hyatt went bankrupt.

When Alfred Sloan, the person who later founded GM, graduated from MIT, he asked his father to buy him Hyatt's small bankrupt business. "Unlike Hyatt," Drucker writes, "Sloan was willing to broaden his vision of the product." The roller bearing was ideal for the emerging automobile business. In two years, Sloan had a flourishing business, with Henry Ford as his biggest customer.

Get out of the box.

Think in whole new ways.

In his new book, *Weird Ideas That Work: 11-1/2 Practices for Promoting, Managing, and Sustaining Innovation,* Stanford professor Robert Sutton reminds readers that people often say they want innovation. They may say it, but they can't get away from their deeply ingrained belief and practices about how to treat people, make decisions, and organize work. Innovation doesn't have a chance unless you're ready to think out of the box.

Growth specialist Aldonna Ambler, CMC, CSP, believes that tough times are the times to really explore what needs doing that isn't being done, or could be done better. "Real wealth is made during recessions," Ambler believes. "The real entrepreneur shines, finds new products or services, and makes the alliances that make it happen." Rather than look for someone to buy you, she continues, start looking for an acquisition you might make. "A company looking to be acquired is a company looking for a CEO," Ambler has found.

If you can lead people to think in new ways about their work, the company, and the products or services it provides, you are well on your way to stability. First, you get out of the box.

Create a Shared Vision

"You have to have internal leaders talking with each other," turnaround specialist Rudy Uribe insists, "Otherwise you can't complete the other actions essential for viability." Too often, Uribe finds, organizational leaders are so busy taking care of their own business units that they don't get together to talk over the big picture.

Multiple locations make it easier for leaders not to be fully aware of what's going on at other locations. It's the same for different departments within the organization. Unless you're a small company where every employee works in the same room, getting people together can be tough.

Part of getting together is to remind leaders that they are in it together. Each person's perspective is often just part of the picture. What's needed is a shared vision.

"Without the shared vision," Uribe has found, "the leadership group doesn't really know where they are going. You might have one leader taking his unit in one direction, while another leader shoves his group toward a different goal. The vision must be a common, shared vision."

Usually that vision is to do the things needed to survive and return to profitability.

"Each leader in an organization thinks he or she has the answer," Uribe often finds, "but they're only looking at a little piece of the picture. They're not seeing the big picture. And too often, they're not working toward the same vision."

Shared visions can be created several ways. Here are three.

1. Put the leaders into a room and don't let them out until they've come up with a vision statement.

Don't bring in extra food; they'll get hungry and work faster. Don't let them take breaks; they'll be more focused. Turn off all cell phones; they might panic. Continue to focus on a vision statement that is agreed upon by all.

It doesn't have to be a long, complicated statement. We mean a shared vision statement that gets right to the point: something like, "Our goal is to return to viability," or "Our vision is to turn red ink into black," or "Our vision is a company that turns a profit this next calendar year." It doesn't matter if you call it your Mission, Goal, or Vision. What is important is that all within the organization share it.

It must be clear and concise so that future actions of the individual leaders can be compared to the shared vision. If the vision is "We will turn red ink into black ink," then all actions can be compared to that vision. If a proposed action doesn't support the vision, then don't do it.

2. Do a Futures Invention or Scenario Planning process.

Ask the leaders or employees to review the trends of the past five years. Then ask them to project out the numbers over the next five or ten years, if zero things are changed within the organization. For example, if there are zero changes in marketing and sales, what will the numbers be? Based on the past three years, if there are zero changes in what and how we do things, what will costs per unit of product/service be? Based on the past several years, if the organization makes zero changes in processes, what will the profit be?

This Futures Invention process asks you to

a. Review the trends of the past several years,
b. Project what the results will be in the next three to five years if ZERO changes occur, and
c. Calculate the numbers (sales, profits, revenue, whatever).

The process often reveals more than some people want. If you chart it out and make it visual, the impact is even greater. See Figure 11-1 for an example.

Figure 11-1. Chart of Futures Invention

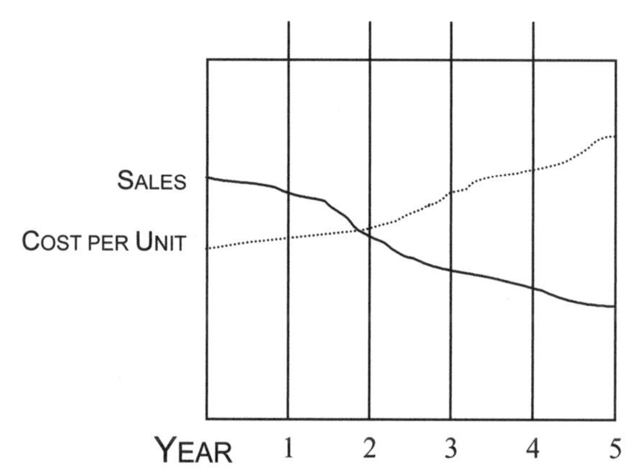

"When we did this, it was easy for us to see where our efforts needed to go," recalls one executive of a $300 million-plus organization. "The exercise made it more clear where we needed to focus our attention. Our projections showed increased costs and a rapidly declining customer base. It made us realize that we needed to make some drastic changes. The changes we ultimately made enabled us to create new markets and new customers with marginal investments. We grew, while many of our competitors declined," the executive adds.

The Futures Invention process can make problem areas more clear so that leaders can turn things around.

3. Do a Future Search.

In the Future Search process, as we mentioned in an earlier chapter, you bring together large groups of people. And the group includes all stakeholders. This means customers and vendors, as well as employees. You can bring together either the whole employee group, or let work units select representatives from each team. Caution: this group of stakeholders is not a handpicked group of people who will agree with whatever leaders say. It must be either the total employee group, or representatives from each team, elected by each team.

In small groups of six to eight people, discussion focuses on the following three questions. They can be discussed separately or all at the same time.

a. What is the future we want?
b. What do we believe in?
c. Why do we exist?

The small groups continue their discussions until they reach informal consensus. Then these small groups are folded into larger groups and the process continues. The normative group process continues until you are finally working with one large group, trying to find consensus for the questions. By the time people have struggled with these three questions and worked through differences, participants are much clearer about their shared vision.

A shared vision enables leaders to work together as a team.

Work as a Team

There's no place for competitive egos in a turnaround situation, states Rudy Uribe. "Make sure you're competing against competitors, not against yourself," he adds. No single leader does it all. Leadership is shared. And people are successful because there are others getting their work done. In other words, you don't turn around an organization by yourself. It takes everybody: a team.

"I like to find people who've been previously misused in the organization," workout specialist David Slaughter advises, "people who've never been supported or encouraged." These people know what's going on, Slaughter believes, and they know what it takes to turn things around. It's just that no one listened to them before or asked for their help.

"I like to get them working as a team, and give them the opportunity to produce results almost immediately," Slaughter adds. People come alive. Things get done. And often solutions for major problems seem to come out of nowhere.

Uribe recalls an assignment to help turn around a retail operation with outlets in three states. The company had lost money for the previous four years. One of the things he found was that the several regional general managers (GMs) were highly competitive with each other. It was even to the point that if one GM needed extra people to service customers in a store, the others wouldn't give up anyone, even for a few days, even across town.

Uribe finally convinced three of the GMs that by working together as a team, sharing their own individual expertise, everyone would benefit. The three GMs headed to each store in their regions to see what differences they could make. One GM was great at showing employees how to provide exemplary customer service. That's what he did in each store. Another GM could take a look at revenue and expenses and find ways to cut costs while not affecting quality or service. That's what he did in each store. And the third GM was great at getting the backroom people performing at high levels. And that's what he did.

The company is making its first profit in four years.

If you have to turn around an operation, you must get people working together as a team, with a shared, common vision.

Share the Glory

What do you do when things are turning around? You thank the people who are making it happen! And those people go well beyond the executive group. Sure, you may have orchestrated the turnaround, but you didn't make it happen in isolation. It happened only because there were good people around you.

"I always give employees the credit," reports retail manager Mike Gold. "After all, they were the ones who met the customers, did the work, saw to it that things were ready when they needed to be ready," he adds. "No manager ever does it by himself," Gold continues, "and if the people did their jobs and it made you look good, then you do what's right—you share the glory and let them know their great work is appreciated," he advises.

Here are three guidelines to share the glory.

1. Share the glory on the spot.

OK, so Team D hit projected goals for the first time in six months. Don't wait until your annual appreciation dinner. Tell them "Thanks!" now. Share the glory the moment the statistics are out. Waiting until the end of the month for a special rewards dinner doesn't help performance at all.

So you tell them, "Hey, thanks, you did great work!" when you first learn about their achievement. Everybody will smile, pat themselves on their backs, and bask in the sunlight of having made a difference.

See somebody doing something extraordinary? Tell them—on the spot.

2. Let others know about it.

Not only tell people on the spot "Thanks for your great work," but let others know about it, too. Put it in a memo to all units, or the weekly newsletter, or e-mail others. You can even make a small sign and post it in their work area, as in Figure 11-2.

Figure 11-2. Sample Sign

It's nice to be told "Thanks!" in person. But it's also nice to know that others know you and your team did good work. There are lots of ways to share the glory by letting others know about people's great work.

3. Get out of the box in ways to share the glory.

Thank you signs and e-mails are great. But sometimes you need to get out of the box to share the glory. You could

- Bring in pizza for everybody.
- Provide tickets for the hottest movie in town.
- Tell people to come to work dressed as a clown.
- Take employees to a sports event.
- Have a family picnic.
- Send people home at noon.
- Send people gift certificates for their favorite restaurants.
- Have flowers for everybody's work areas.

When things start turning around, share the glory. You didn't do it by yourself!

Don't Rest on Your Laurels

What do you do when you get things turned around and the company is making a profit? You sure don't sit back, or take a long vacation. In today's business world, leaders need to continue to lead to be sure their organizations remain healthy. Leaders can't rest on their laurels.

Dutch Boy® paints is a good example. They were doing well, making a profit. Even in down times, people need to paint their houses or remodel instead of buying new. Even the new home market continues to do well, with the lowest mortgage rates for decades. So things were good at Dutch Boy. And then someone started brainstorming to make things even better. For nearly 100 years, paint had been distributed in round, metal cans. That's just the way it was. And who of us hasn't said a few words as we tried to pour paint into a roller pan, only to have it go all over the can? Or yelled out loud when the paint sprayed over the floor as we tried to put the lid back on?

But Dutch Boy is changing the way consumers buy paint. Their Twist and Pour™ container is square. It doesn't waste space. It has a nice, comfortable handle, not a thin wire that cuts into your hands. It comes complete with its own pouring spout. If you've painted as many walls as we have, then you'd get excited, too, at this dramatic innovation.

Dutch Boy was doing well. They weren't in financial trouble. But they didn't want to rest on their laurels; they just wanted to do better. So they got out of the box, worked together, and shared the vision of improving product usability.

Once you get things moving the way you want to, don't sit back. Don't say, "Yeah, I know we need to look at new services, but..." "Sure, we need to make certain we're ready for new markets, but..." or even, "Yes, I could do more, but...."

A lot of good companies slide downhill on their "buts."

Make sure yours doesn't.

* * *

"As workers become increasingly proficient at playing the game of business, they change the game. They set their aspirations higher."

(Tom Ehrenfeld)

Chapter Twelve: How Do I Restore Confidence?

What do you do when you're asked to step in and take charge and there are lots of things that need fixing? Morale is low. Regulators are all over the place. Media asks lots of questions. And the cat is pregnant again.

It's a tough time. Your task is to step in and restore confidence in the company, the leadership, and the products or services. You have to be open and friendly. And yet you still have to deal with all the stuff that's been going on, even if you didn't know anything about it beforehand. So do it. Here are seven actions you can take to make the transition smoother.

1. Communicate
2. Be accessible
3. Listen
4. Share all the details
5. Engage the people
6. Turn bad press into good press
7. Work with integrity

By taking these actions, you establish yourself as a key leader and begin to make a difference.

Communicate

Communication is the key to making things whole again. Without it, you'll never be an effective leader, and the tough times will just get tougher. To be truly effective, your communication must be more than just a weekly memo or e-mail to employees. It needs to be in person.

Remember Mel Rambo from Section One? "You need to communicate with your people, let them know things are going to work out OK," states the National Travelers Life president. And the best way to do this, Rambo found out, is through direct contact.

"In smaller companies, you can hold meetings with all your employees at once," Rambo states. That way everyone hears the same thing at the same time. In larger companies, group meetings with each business unit can accomplish about the same thing.

The important thing is to communicate—everything. Communicate everything about the company that employees want to know. Things like

- New directions, new goals
- Plans to make corrections
- Costs
- Revenues
- Losses
- Profits
- Stock prices
- 401(K)s

It takes less time for wounds to heal when communication is frequent and direct. And communication helps to rebuild trust. It's like adding an antibiotic to a festering sore. As a leader in a tough situation, you'll find that the more you directly communicate with the people, the quicker there are solutions, confidence gets restored, and people lead so that others can follow.

When Herb Baum took over as chair and CEO of The Dial Corporation, he called all the employees together. It was announced that Baum would be moving from a position on the board of directors to the chair and CEO role. "There will be some changes," Baum stated. "First, if you can't be nice to others, there's no place for you within Dial." He paused. No one left. So he continued.

You've no doubt noticed that communication is mentioned throughout this book. It is a major part of leading in tough times. It is a major foundation for responsibility, trust, and motivation. By mentioning it over and over, it's our way of saying that without effective communication, as direct communication as you can provide, it will be impossible to restore confidence in the leadership or the organization, or establish yourself as a leader in tough times.

Here are even more ways to communicate directly with your people:

- *E-mail.* Send periodic or regular updates through the organization's intranet system, keeping people informed as to what is taking place and the progress made.

- *Newsletters.* Public periodic or regular updates, which can focus not only on the organization's progress, but can also highlight people and teams who have made significant contributions.

- *Voice mail.* Leave a VM for a person, thanking them for doing an exceptional job, or letting them know you appreciate their extra hours, or whatever. A personal VM from my leader that I can listen to in the morning is very impressive. It makes me glad to be part of the organization.
- *Huddles.* Be part of a work team's morning huddle, when people gather around in a circle (standing) and take 10 to 12 minutes to talk about who's doing what, what people accomplished yesterday, what they are looking forward to today, and who needs what kind of help. Fill them in on the organization's progress, problems, and challenges.
- *Individual meetings.* Set a schedule to meet each week with several work teams. Listen to their concerns. Ask for solutions. Share your ideas, frustrations, and the progress that's been made in restoring confidence.

The quickest way to restore confidence is to be visible, ready to talk with anyone, and willing to talk directly with the media. Without direct communication, there is no restoring confidence.

Be Accessible

Part of communication is being accessible. Too many leaders sit in their offices with people around them to keep others out. They park their cars in a special place, away from employees. Meals are sent in. They don't show up at training sessions. They make a cameo appearance at the company picnic. But that's it.

It's no wonder that employees want to know what's going on.

The second action for stepping in as a new leader is to be accessible. "One of the first things Mel Rambo did," reports one of his leadership team, "was to keep his office door open. He'd get to the office at 7 a.m., and people knew they could stop by and talk with him about anything."

At noon, Mel would eat lunch in the company cafeteria. He would walk around the office during the day, saying hello to people and asking how things were going. He'd answer questions as best he could. And sometimes he'd have to say, "I don't know yet how we're going to handle that." And he was open to possible solutions. Often he would ask, "What do you think we could do?" And then he'd listen.

Gary Bertch doesn't have to restore confidence. But he knows how to maintain it. He walks around, talking with people, finding out what's going on in their lives and also what's going on in their work unit.

People like to see him out on the lines. It makes them realize they are important parts of the organization.

Growth specialist Aldonna Ambler reminds leaders that in tough times, employees are looking for every hint they can find that things will be OK. Employees want to be reassured that the sacrifices they've made will have a payback, and that the leaders are working hard to turn things around. You don't restore confidence by staying in your office, shutting the door, and having meetings with people in suits and white shirts and red ties. You restore confidence by being visible. After all, if you're visible and accessible, then things are obviously going to be all right.

Listen

As a person moves up the leadership scale from supervisor to manager to director to vice president, listening plays an increasing role. Listening specialist Betsy McKnight Latko reports that over 60 percent of a leader's day is spent listening. The rest of the time, the leader is doing.

If you're trying to restore confidence, you'll find yourself listening a lot more than talking—or at least that's the way it should be. It's only by listening that you find out the concerns of your people, your customers, and the public.

Here are seven ways you can enhance your listening skills.

1. Listen for main ideas.

In an environment where confidence is being restored, some people who want your attention might use emotional triggers in their conversations. Perhaps their tone is confrontive. Maybe they use emotionally charged phrases such as, "Well, if they had only…" or "This really didn't need to happen…" or even "What a bunch of crap this is." Don't let tones or words set you off, or push your emotional buttons. Listen for the main ideas behind the emotion. Then you can deal with it.

2. Ask for clarification.

Sometimes you're not sure what you're hearing, so ask for clarification. "It would really help me if you could explain that last comment," or "Now, I think this is what I heard…. Is that what you intended?" If what you heard isn't what the person intended, then continue the discussion until both are clear about what the other said.

3. Follow up with action.

Let the speaker know that you're going to do something about the message: "I'll get back to you by Friday," or "Great idea, let's both add some detail and meet on Wednesday morning at 10 a.m." Action indicates that you listened and understood. I listened, I thought, I acted.

4. Ask provocative questions.

Ask questions that make the person think: "It seems to me such an action would be helpful for the CEO. How do you think we can best present it?" Use questions to lead others to solutions: "Well, if we follow your recommendation, will it also affect costs?" Buy-in and commitment are stronger when employees are part of decision-making.

5. Step into the other person's world.

The "walk in your shoes" phrase is outworn, but it's not worn out. It still applies. Sometimes to really understand what the other person is saying, we have to try to put ourselves in that person's world. Our point of view could change with the additional input.

6. Listen to what is not said.

Nonverbal communication, including tone of voice, sends crucial messages. Pay attention to it. Saying "Wow, great idea" while you stare at the floor with drooping shoulders suggests that maybe you aren't being honest. Or at least aren't really sold on the idea. Eye contact and relaxed or tense shoulder set are nonverbal messages that need to be heard.

7. Ask more of yourself.

OK, it's late in the afternoon, you've been in your office since 7:05 a.m., and here comes Sherry who wants to talk about becoming a team leader. Ask more of yourself. If you're trying to restore confidence, it's imperative that you listen to just about all those who want, or need, to talk with you. That's what being a leader is all about. You do some things because they are the right thing to do. Don't just listen when it is convenient. Be a model listener for others. The best way to get others to listen to you is to first listen to them.

Share All the Details

"It was no fun," states Melanie K. Arntsen, Ph.D., former Arthur Andersen employee, "but if you're a manager you have to be informed.

And you have to keep your people informed, too." That means sharing the details. "Our leaders tried very hard to make sure that employees knew things before we read about it in the newspapers," Arntsen continues.

When you're trying to restore confidence with your employees and your customers, you need to share all the details—the good, the bad, and the ugly—but mostly the good. In Chapter 11, we wrote about opening the books and sharing all the information there is to share. It's the same to restore confidence. "If you suffocate people," Mike Gold believes, "they simply don't respond very well." And without information, you suffocate people.

What kind of information do you share as you strive to restore confidence?

- All the efforts you and others are taking to put things back in order again
- The results of all those efforts
- The checks and balances that are being instituted
- The financials, all of them—based on the business savvy of your people
- What the media is saying and your response
- Just about anything that a valued employee wants to hear
- Just about anything a valued customer would want to know

As we've said before, communication is a very basic skill and activity for leading in tough times. This means listening, sharing information, and never letting an employee hear it on the evening news before hearing it from you!

A few years ago, we were working with a bank that was about to be merged. There were lots of rumors in the mid-sized city, and the bank's 700-plus employees were wondering what was going to happen not only to the bank, but to them. The executive vice president, realizing how the people were wanting to be kept in the loop, started a weekly Merger Update newsletter to all employees.

Sometimes all it said was, "Nothing more has happened since last week." Other weeks it took two or three pages to detail all that was going on. The people loved it. They at least knew they were getting all the details and before it was printed in the morning paper. Key to restoring confidence is sharing all the details.

Your people won't understand all the details? Then provide business literacy sessions so that they know how companies make money, what a P&L statement means, and how to measure ROI. It's only when employees have the details that they can begin thinking about ways to make it better.

Engage the People

It's not enough that you are working hard at restoring confidence. You need to engage your people, too. After all, they are in it with you. They are also stakeholders in what takes place. Like you, the leader, it is in their best interest to see the organization's reputation back where it was. Here are five actions you can take.

1. Create solutions.

One of the characteristics that is different between high performance organizations and those just muddling along is the involvement of employees. High performance organizations involve their people each day in creating solutions. We like the basic question, "What needs doing that isn't being done, or could be done better?" It's catchy and easy for employees to remember. Chapter 8 describes how you can make use of this question in creating needed change. You can also ask this question in relation to restoring confidence.

Show your people how they can go through their workday, looking for ways to create solutions. Let them identify how they will process all the information gathered and how they will present their recommended actions. Establish the expectation that your people create solutions, and show them your confidence in this new skill set.

2. Use short-term task forces.

Short-term task forces can be very effective in coming up with solutions to organizational problems. Pull together a team of people (or task force) and charge them with finding solutions to a specific issue—not a whole bunch of issues, but one specific problem that needs to be resolved.

You can either ask them to come back with three recommendations or the single best solution. Part of it depends on the make-up of your task force. If the group has a tendency to get sucked into "analysis-paralysis," then ask them to come up with the three best options to resolve the issue and the pros and cons of each. Then the appropriate people can make the final decision, based on the task force's recommendations.

But keep the task forces small—no more than seven people. And keep the total an odd number—three, five, or seven. If the task force is too large, it becomes cumbersome and wastes too much time giving each person a time to talk. When the group is small, it is easier to build consensus and to come back with the anticipated recommendations.

Make the task forces short term. They have one and only one assignment. It will take a few days or a few weeks, at most, for them to complete their assignment. Using short-term task forces allows you to pull together people with the special skills you need for a single assignment.

3. Form synergistic groups.

Many organizations have used the Kolbe technology (see Chapter 8) to form high performance groups. Kolbe's research and the experience of many organizations both large and small clearly show you can put together a team with a high probability of success.

When you know the conative strengths of potential task-force members, you can form a team with just the right amount of probing, organizing, innovating, and demonstrating strengths. The conative differences enable a synergistic group to come up with better solutions than if just one or two of the natural strengths are present in the group. Master Kolbe Consultant Sandra Brownfield Deems states, "Synergistic teams will get things done quicker and with more workable solutions than when you just put people together without any consideration of how they approach problem solving."

4. Report back.

It's not enough just to take recommendations from a task force. You must report back on what is happening with their recommendations. If the task force presented three possible solutions, and the key decision makers have narrowed it to one, let the group know which one and why. If none of their recommendations are further considered, let them know why.

The quickest way to shut down employee creativity and synergy is to ask them to do something and then never report back as to the outcomes. One of the primary ways you develop a vital workplace is to engage your people in finding solutions and then tell them what's happened to their recommendations.

5. Train people in problem solving.

By the time we've reached adulthood, we've solved thousands of problems. But few of us have ever been trained in any problem-solving process. We just do it. When you train people in a basic problem-solving approach, you increase their confidence in coming up with workable solutions.

It doesn't need to be a complicated problem-solving paradigm. We like the basic five-step approach:

Step 1. What is the real problem to be solved? Sometimes the initial problem that brings the group together isn't the real problem, but only an indication. Example: Turnover in IT is high. Is it because you can't find good IT people or because the IT manager doesn't know how to lead people?

Step 2. What are all the possible solutions? Brainstorming, benchmarking from other organizations, and searching the literature are all ways to identify possible solutions. We like to see as many possible strategies identified as possible. An idea can always be discarded as not workable. But if you omit possible solutions, you might be walking away from the one that's right for your situation.

Step 3. Of all the possible solutions, which one/ones will resolve the issue in the most effective way, fit within the workplace culture, and serve to fulfill the organization's mission? Example: One way to increase cash flow is to not pay selected vendors. It's a solution, but one that is contrary to most workplace cultures and doesn't fulfill the organization's mission. Step 3 often involves a great deal of time and dialogue among the task force members.

Step 4. Make the selection and implement. Make your decision and put your decision into action.

Step 5. Continually evaluate the solution and refine as needed. It's hard to foretell every contingency, and often solutions need to be fine-tuned once they are in place. Anticipate it, and plan for it.

Several years ago, we were talking with a CEO about how his privately owned company was organized and how decisions were made. "I don't have time to know everything," the CEO stated, "so I trust those who are doing the work to let me know what needs to happen." He knew how to involve his people.

Turn Bad Press into Good Press

Nobody likes to read negative things about their organization in the newspaper or hear about it on the evening news. But sometimes it happens. It's usually not because of things you did, but because of things someone else did. But as a leader in tough times, you're the person to deal with it. Your task is to turn bad press into good, not only for your organization's customers, but also for your employees. Here's how you can do it.

First, understand that the media isn't "out to get you." No matter how unfair you may think the negative press is, it doesn't do you or your investors or your employees any good to blame the media for what they're saying. "There really are very few occasions where the media is actually out to get you," reports non-profit executive Phyllis Lepke. "It does no good to accuse the press of this kind of treatment," Lepke continues, "and your constituents will have a hard time believing that some reporter made up the whole story."

The media's role is to report "news" and to be factual about it. Part of your task as a leader is to make sure the media has the correct information.

Second, establish ties with the media. Be assertive. Ask to meet with reporters, editors, and TV news schedulers (the people who decide what is and what isn't aired). Get acquainted with them *before* they call. Share what's going on within your organization and be ready to candidly answer any question that you are asked. "Share your philosophy, your values, what's going on and why," Lepke counsels. "It makes it more clear to reporters what's really going on," she adds.

And it makes it easier for reporters to decide if there's a story.

Add reporters to your regular communication list. You can even send them newsletters that your company sends to employees and customers. And be sure they receive press releases about special events within your organization: awards, new patents, new products or services, new location, new personnel, and on and on. Invite them to come to your site, and give them a tour. Let them talk with employees, other leaders, and anyone they want to talk with. And then ask them again if there's anything else they'd like to know about you.

Third, ask your media contacts what you can do to help them do their job. They will usually be appreciative and tell you specifically what will help them the most. They might tell you that they only want press releases when there's something big taking place. Or they might ask to be on your newsletter list or want a copy of your annual report. Just provide them with what they ask for.

What if they ask for information that's proprietary, or if you're not yet ready to talk about a new product or service? Then acknowledge the validity of their question and carefully explain that this is something you can't talk about now, but you will in the near future. Offer to call them first when you announce it—build relationships.

Fourth, be accessible. If a reporter calls, answer the phone. Answer their questions directly and to the point. If you hesitate, protest too much, or try to evade answering a fair question, their ears perk up. A good reporter will "know that here's a story," and then they'll push you. Remember, that's their job.

And finally, take media training. If you're the person who deals with the press, then take a course on working with the press. There are media consultants in every major city, people who know how to work effectively with the media. Often, they are former radio, newspaper, or TV reporters. They know how the media works. They know how reporters will try to get under your skin. And they can help you learn how to turn bad press into good press.

Former pro-football player turned bank executive Tommy Vaughn tells a classic story in how to turn negative press into positive press. Vaughn had been named president of a Southside Chicago bank only a few months earlier. As he drove into the bank's parking lot one morning, he saw a crowd of people standing in front of the bank. Some had placards.

It was a protest, complete with chants and people marching in front of the bank. The protest, Vaughn discovered, was because several community people believed the bank wasn't doing all it could to provide small business loans and home mortgages for people in the community. Tommy listened intently as the people made their demands. "I understand," he said over and over again. Then he went inside, made a few phone calls, and took a card table and a few folding chairs out to the sidewalk. Pretty soon a truck came up with boxes of donuts and pots of coffee and Vaughn laid them out on the card table. "Help yourself," he invited the protesters, "it's chilly and the coffee will keep you warm. And who can turn down a good donut?"

As he stepped back into the bank, there were TV reporters holding on lines 1 and 2 and a newspaper reporter on line 3. "Yes," he told them all, "there's a demonstration going on in front of the bank. The people think the bank hasn't worked hard enough at providing loans and mortgages," he volunteered.

Then he said to each reporter, "Why don't you come on down and talk with the people yourself? Have a cup of coffee and a donut. And you can listen to what the people have to say." Nobody showed up. Because Vaughn was so open with the information, there obviously wasn't a real story.

Pretty soon the protestors started going home. Tommy had listened, provided coffee and donuts, and obviously was going to do what he could to fix the problem. And Tommy Vaughn established the reputation with the media, and his customers, as being fair, open, and ready to talk. They all became his allies in his community development work.

As a leader in tough times, you can turn negative press into positive press.

Work with Integrity

In Chapter 7, we wrote that working with integrity is being consistent in living out your values. It also means that people can trust you to tell the truth. You don't say one thing in one situation, and then turn around and say something else to another person or group. Be consistent and have integrity.

Without integrity—without doing your work so that people trust what you are saying—you can never restore confidence. Here's an example. A direct mail marketing company we were working with had recently been sold. About 20 percent of its workforce was eliminated. As WorkLife Design began its job transition program, we were asked to come to an early morning meeting to hear the president of the acquiring company. He was making his first appearance in person. He was tall, handsome, and well groomed. There was lots of coffee and sodas and pastries.

The mood was pretty upbeat. Then he began his speech: "We're pleased to have made this acquisition of such a fine company," he began. And then he did it. "I just want you to know," he said, "that there will be no more change. Our downsizing is over, and there will be no more changes here for a long, long time."

The people knew better. There are always changes when one company acquires another. We listened and observed, and heard employees chuckling among themselves. Several even got up and walked out. "What's he going to do?" asked one person on the way out, "fire me?" Within three months, there were other major reorganizations and job eliminations at the facility. But even before then, morale had declined. Productivity hit the skids. The acquiring company had no integrity. The president never showed up again.

And those he sent to run the acquired business were never really trusted. People never knew if what was being said was accurate or not. Confidence plummeted. The organization never fully recovered.

It would have been much better had the president announced that these were the first changes to take place. That other adjustments would be made in the next six months. Then he could have explained what some of the changes might be. He could have projected a timeline so that people knew when changes might be coming. People would have at least believed him. They may not have liked it, but they would have respected it. People want honesty and integrity. It goes a lot further than trying to tell employees what you think they want to hear.

Trying to tell employees that everything is just great when it isn't—and the employees know it isn't—is lousy leadership. In fact, it's not leadership at all. Employees want honesty—the truth. They can deal with the truth. Even if it isn't what they want to hear. But at least they know, and they know they haven't been given a snow job.

You restore confidence by walking the talk, by being honest, by being up front.

Some days all you have as a leader is your integrity. If you really want to restore confidence in the organization, then be open and honest, with your people, the press, shareholders, and other leaders.

* * *

"At the core of every business problem is a people problem.
And most of the time people problems are not about the
failure of individual people. It ain't about them. It's about you.
We succeed if our employees succeed."

(Vally M. Sharpe, M.A.)

Chapter Thirteen: How Do I Motivate People in Tough Times?

The company's been losing money. There was some bad press, both TV and newspaper, right after the downsizing. Two people filed wrongful termination suits against the company. The board replaced two CEOs in three years. Your task? Keep the people happy and productive. Keep people motivated.

That's why you've spent hours reading about motivation. The company spent big bucks for a three-day motivation seminar in Boston. You benchmarked other organizations. It all helps. But we have found the most productive approach to helping people stay motivated is to ask them, from entry level on up, focused questions. Why do they stay? Why are they willing to put in extra hours? Why are some willing to miss family events, like soccer games and school plays, just to finish a project on time? Why do some come in early or stay late? Do you really want to know? Ask them.

Here are five questions you can ask. The answers you receive will help you know how to lead others through tough times.

1. Why Are You Working?

Think it's an easy question? Then why are you working? What do *you* get from it? What's important to you about your work? Sure, we need a job to pay bills. But there's Sherry, whose big house is paid for, whose kids are grown, and who wears expensive clothes. I wonder why she works. Or Ken, who's been caught in two downsizings. Or Tish, a young mother with another one on the way. Or Alice, whose husband is retired. Why do people work?

Psychotherapist turned leadership consultant Vally M. Sharpe states:

> *In my experience we all work for different reasons at different times in our lives, and why we work at any given time significantly impacts how much energy we can commit to a job. If you work to make ends meet so you can spend time with your family, that's one thing. If you work to achieve and maintain a certain standard of living, that's another. If you work because*

> *what you do is a large part of your identity, that's still another. And what is true for you now may not have been true 10 years ago, nor will it be true 10 years from now.*

Each of these motivations is legitimate for the person. But each has a different impact on the time and energy a person is willing to give to the job. What you need to do is take the time to learn why your people work. When you understand why each one works, you can adjust your leadership actions according to each person's reason for working.

If a person is just getting started in a career, maybe that person is ready to put in extra hours, come in on Saturday morning, stay late two or more evenings a week. After all, that's how the person gets established. This person will thrive on added responsibilities, new learnings, and new experiences. Provide them.

If a person is working just to pay bills and keep the family together, then you probably have a 9-to-5 person—in not much before 9:00, and gone by 5:05. You have their full attention while they're on the job, but their real motivation is to have extra dollars so that the kids can get new clothes, the extra bedroom can be added on, and there's money left over for new tires for the car.

If a person is working because that's his or her identity, then they'll be ready to do things that further their career, add to their exposure, and help establish them as authorities in their field. Extra projects are welcome, as long as there is extra visibility and recognition.

Sandra likes to solve problems—different kinds of problems. Give her a problem to solve, the resources to solve it, and a reasonable timeline to get it solved, and Sandra is ecstatic. Take problem solving away from her, and she'll walk.

Unless you talk with people and listen to their words and the emotions beneath their words, you won't have a clue to why they work. And if you don't know why they work, and how much energy they are willing to commit to work at any given time, you won't know how to lead them in tough times. You won't know how to adjust your planning, who to assign what, and when to back off from asking for too much from some people.

A number of years ago, Richard was talking with Don Clifton, founder of Selection Research Inc., now Gallup. Clifton's early research was some of the basic foundation for the best seller, *First, Break All the Rules* (Marcus Buckingham and Curt Coffman, Simon & Schuster, 1999). Richard was talking with Clifton about a position at SRI, and Don wanted to know the best way to compensate him.

"I want to buy a house," Richard explained, "because I'm tired of living in apartments." OK, said Clifton, we'll provide you with the down payment for a house. "I've driven used cars for so long," Richard continued, "and I'd somehow like a new car." We can do that, Clifton responded. The company will lease you a new car each year. And on it went.

Clifton had discovered early that you don't treat all the people the same way. We work for different reasons. We want different things from our work. Unless you take time to talk with people, you won't know why they work or what they want from it. The first part of motivating people in tough times is to find out why they work.

Ask your people why they work. You'll gain great insight into how to be their most effective leader. But first, use Activity 13-1 to ask yourself why you work and what you have wanted from work over the years.

Activity 13-1. Why I Work

Why I work today…

____

____

____

What I wanted from work 5 years ago…

____

____

____

What I wanted from work 10 years ago…

____

____

____

(Take it as far back as your first real job)

____

____

____

2. What Don't You Know That You Want to Know?

You hire people because of what they know. But in order to maximize their potential, you have to find out what they don't know and what they want to learn. Sometimes what they want to learn is fairly simple, like explaining why you changed the schedule. Or it may be more sophisticated, like wanting to learn the new software system that will cut paperwork in half. But first, the leader needs to know.

When times get tough, leaders sometimes cut back on the one thing they need most: training and learning programs. It's often the first thing that gets cut when times are tough. It should be the last. Result: Employees can't succeed because they don't know what they need to know.

Sure, it's an easy place to cut the budget, so learning programs get cut. Forget about that Supervisors 101 program. Let them find it out on their own. Forget about the program on Making Change Work. People will just have to learn to survive this last reorganization on their own. And so we end up wasting money fixing things that didn't have to break if only the right training had been provided. Or sometimes people move on because there's no opportunity to learn and grow.

Melissa had been a successful supervisor and team leader, and was ready to move into a manager's position. She accepted the promotion with lots of enthusiasm and energy, but it wasn't as easy as she thought. She asked for help: a management coach, or taking a class at the area community college, or bringing in someone to help her and others learn important management skills. But the suggestion was declined—it was too costly and would keep Melissa from getting other things done.

So Melissa made some mistakes in leading her team and kept a new financial product from being rolled out on time. And then she left. She found a job where they would provide the kind of learning she wanted and needed. And her former company lost their investment in bringing Melissa to the point where she was, all because they thought it would cost too much. Now it will cost them between 75 and 110 percent of her annual compensation to recruit, select, hire, train, and bring up to speed someone to replace her.

Tough times are the times to increase investments in learning, not shut them down. There are other ways to cut costs. Turn off a few lights. Buy used furniture. Reduce country club memberships or other perks that don't add a direct value.

What do you want to learn? And what do your people want to learn? Complete Activity 13-2 to help define what you/your people want to learn.

Activity 13-2. What Do I/My People Want to Learn

What I want to learn...	What my people want to learn...
______________	______________
______________	______________
______________	______________
______________	______________
______________	______________
______________	______________
______________	______________

When you know what your people want to know—what they want to learn—then you're well on your way to motivating others in tough times.

3. What Kind of Workplace Do You Want?

The next question focuses on the kind of workplace where people can be fully productive and satisfied at the same time. Does it exist? Yes, in lots of places. People are glad to come to work in the morning. There isn't a crush to get out the doors at the end of the day. People share differences of opinion without malice. Workers are friends with one other.

At WorkLife Design, we've asked thousands of people to identify employers of choice in their cities—places where people *want* to work. Then we asked them to give three reasons why those places are employers of choice. This is what we've learned.

Pay. Only 34 percent of respondents said pay was one of the most important parts of being an employer of choice. That doesn't mean that you can pay the lowest wage in town. It just means that after a point, pay is not the most important thing in a job.

What people did say was that pay needed to be fair, equitable, and marketable. You don't pay men more than women for the same job. And you don't pay the top brass hundreds of times more than the average employee makes. To attract and retain the best, we've learned, you need to pay above the mid-point for each job within your market.

If you pay the least for the job in your market, you will not have the recruiting power you need. And people will leave when they can find a job that pays more. It always surprises us when organizations pay the lowest hourly wage for entry-level positions. And then employees leave when they can get 25 cents an hour more across town. It costs the company more than those 25 cents an hour to find and train a new person.

To really be successful in finding and keeping the best people, you need to pay in the top quartile for each job in your market. An IT manager will cost you more in Boston than in Tucson. Why? Because it costs more to live in Boston than in Tucson. And people often measure their income by what's left over after all the bills are paid.

Benefits. More employees were concerned about benefits than pay, and 56 percent of respondents placed benefits as a major reason a company is seen as an employer of choice. Of prime importance was the flexibility of benefit packages. "With both my husband and me working," one woman responded, "there's no need for healthcare insurance from both employers. What I'd really like," she continued, "is the flexibility to have dental and eye care insurance from my employer instead."

Benefits packages with flexibility are popular. Some of it gets back to why people are working. If you have a young family, then healthcare is very important, just as it is when one gets older. For others, the opportunity to contribute extra dollars toward retirement might be favored. And others might want the opportunity to take four-day weekends, rather than take vacation in one-week blocks of time.

Assistance in childcare was another benefit often mentioned. Some employers like SAS have onsite daycare, which employees really like. Others pay part of the costs of daycare as a benefit option. And still other employers keep an up-to-date list of preferred daycare providers for their new employees and new parents.

Some organizations have asked employees what different kinds of benefits would be helpful. For example, a hospital in the Midwest has arranged for employees to drop off grocery shopping lists at the beginning of the shift and pick up the groceries at the end of the shift. Or they can drop off film to be developed in the morning and pick up the pictures in the afternoon. Many organizations are becoming highly imaginative in providing different kinds of benefits. They just ask their people to identify benefits that make it easier for them to be productive.

We noticed a trend in the past few years that employees were opting for benefits that focused on fitness and prevention of illness. An increasing number of employers are providing onsite fitness centers or pay part of an employee's membership in a fitness center. We predict benefits that focus on fitness and health will be increasingly requested.

Workplace Environment. For most people, 82 percent, the workplace environment was what made a company a great place to work. Family friendly and work/life balance were often mentioned as key to being a great place to work. So were trust and cooperation, fairness and respect, credible and fair management, and involved leadership (or servant leadership).

Involved leadership, sometimes called servant leadership, was frequently mentioned. What is it? It's getting involved and helping people get done what needs to get done. Here's an example. A few years ago there was a chain of fast-food restaurants that made use of servant leadership. The role of each manager was to keep track of what was going on within the restaurant and then step in where needed: fry burgers, bus tables, greet customers. If it needed to be done, the manager was supposed to do it—now. The restaurants were very successful, and though they charged more for their food, they had the leading market share.

New owners, however, thought it was pretty costly for managers to be bussing tables during rush hour. That was the job, the new owners said, for the hourly help. The manager's role was changed to a more traditional role. The managers should sit in their office and let the workers do it. It took less than three years for the chain to close its stores.

A few weeks ago, a friend, Sam, stopped in to a local business for a transaction that would only take a few minutes. All the help was busy, but the manager wasn't. From his glass-walled office, he saw Sam waiting. The manager did what he'd obviously been taught to do—he turned to work at his computer so that he didn't have to watch Sam wait. There was no servant leadership, no customer service. Sam wondered if he had made a mistake doing business with that organization.

We also hear employees talking about the workplace being family friendly. Sometimes it's called work/life balance. Employees know they have things that need to get done. They also know that sometimes things can get done early in the morning or at night or even on the weekend. What they want is the flexibility to leave early to watch the kids play soccer. Or take the morning off to visit school. Or take an extended lunchtime so that they can see dad, who just had his first angioplasty.

But too many leaders have a hard time being flexible. Thom had worked most of Saturday and even Sunday afternoons for the past three weeks, just to make sure the IT conversion came in on time. But

Wednesday he mentioned to his boss that he would be taking off at 3:30 in the afternoon so that he could watch his son play soccer. The boss said, "No." It was against policy, he stated. Thom quietly walked over to his desk, picked up his personal belongings, and walked over to his boss's office. "I'm quitting," he said, "I can't afford to work for a place like this."

You want to motivate your people in tough times? That's easy. Just be sure your people have the kind of workplace environment where they can be fully productive and happy at the same time.

4. How Do You Want to Be Managed?

Can you ask that question? Sure you can. And the information you get back enables you to be an exemplary motivator during tough times. Business development consultant Todd McDonald surveyed several thousand employees, asking them to finish the sentence stem, "I wish my manager would just…." Here are the top five responses he received.

Say Thank You. We're taught as children to say "Please," and afterward to smile and say "Thank You." But evidently, a lot of managers forget this basic rule of conduct. People want managers who will stop and take time to say, "Thanks for taking extra time to get that report completed," or "Thanks for sitting in for me at that meeting," or "Thanks for staying an extra hour so that we could finish the data analysis."

McDonald relates that as he was growing up, if any of the kids in his family refused to send a thank you note after receiving a gift, the gift was sent back to the giver. The reason? "The cycle of giving had not been completed because we had not been grateful," McDonald reports.

People just like to hear, "Thank you." It's an acknowledgement that one's efforts are appreciated. Isn't it great that Bob Nelson's book, *1001 Ways to Reward Your Employees,* has sold so many copies?

Tell Me What's Going On. We often use the phrase "knowledge is power." Too often, however, it appears that as leaders we're keeping our people powerless. We don't always tell them what's going on. No wonder they sometimes feel out of the loop. As they go about doing their jobs, they see leaders head off to another meeting. The door to the meeting room closes and nobody comes out for over an hour.

What's going on now? How will it affect me? What impact will that meeting have on my future? My job? My income? "Put yourself in my shoes," people reported to McDonald. "It makes it easier to have energy to do my job, when I'm not worrying about what's coming next."

Make the Hard Decisions. Leaders get paid extra to make hard decisions. And employees want them to do it. Do you have someone who isn't performing as they should? Then decide to do something about it and do it. Do you have to decide between two good people for a new position? Make the decision so that everyone else can move on with their lives and their jobs.

When leaders don't make the hard decisions, employees wonder who's in charge. They lose respect for the leader who can't, or won't, make the tough calls. So go ahead. Make them. Be ready to explain why you decided what you decided. But make the hard decisions when they need to be made.

Ask for Feedback and Take It Seriously. When you ask for feedback you're indicating that you know you don't know it all. And you know that often the best advice comes from the people doing the job. It also acknowledges the worth of the employees' knowledge and experience. It shows that you see their contribution and insight as an integral part of the collective effort.

If you ask for feedback, then act on it. If the feedback doesn't fit, thank the person, and explain why the suggestion or idea won't work in this instance. And then tell them to keep giving you feedback. If the feedback is just what you needed, tell the person. Let others also know how the employee's feedback is helping.

Here are three guidelines for taking people seriously and getting their best ideas:

- Give the person some advance time when asking for ideas and input. "I might know a lot about the subject, but sometimes I have a hard time forming the ideas when I'm on the spot" is a frequently heard comment.
- Listen attentively while the person is talking. Don't let your mind or eyes wander. Listen, acknowledge what the person is saying, and ask clarifying questions if you need to.
- Take the person seriously. If the shared information is usable, tell the employee. Thank the person. If the shared information isn't usable, thank the person and tell them why you can't use their idea. They will still be ready to share ideas the next time you ask.

Ask for feedback. Listen to it. Consider it. You'll learn lots!

Acknowledge I Have a Personal Life. People know that while they're at work, they need to get their tasks completed. But each person comes to work each day thinking about family, friends, kids, money, and all kinds of other personal things. They have a life.

And their other concerns don't simply go away when they walk through the doors at the beginning of their workday. They bring their personal life with them: sick kids, bills to pay, tension with in-laws, arguments over how to spend money, note from the teacher, worry about parent's health. "Most employees know they have to get things done," McDonald finds, "but they want you to acknowledge that sometimes family matters are what's foremost on their mind."

Leaders need to acknowledge that every employee has a personal life. And sometimes, people want you to be flexible enough so that they have time and energy to do their work and deal with personal issues that need their attention, too.

5. How Am I Doing?

The fifth question you can ask your people is, "How am I doing as a leader?" If you've asked the other questions first, you will get some good feedback with this question. What you're looking for is feedback on your leadership skills and whether or not you're putting in place the contingencies by which people can choose to motivate themselves.

Motivate themselves? Yes.

We believe that no one can motivate another person. A leader can't, in any sustainable way at least, motivate you to stay late, or make sure the job gets done, or go the extra mile. All he or she can do is set up the contingencies by which you choose to motivate yourself. That's why all those questions should be asked. Once the leader knows why you work, what you don't know that you want to know, what kind of workplace you want, and how you want to be led, then the leader knows what contingencies to put in place so that you can choose to motivate yourself.

Executive coach Gail McDonald puts it this way:

> *When we talk about motivation we usually mean people willing to give more than they thought they could. They go the extra mile. But motivation comes from the inside, not the outside. People decide, themselves, to give that extra effort to an organization or cause. What we can do is take the actions, which increase the opportunities for people to give that "extra effort."*

All we can do is set up the contingency by which people choose to motivate themselves. It only follows, then, that motivating in tough times is based on knowing how you're doing in setting up those contingencies.

Here are three ways you can get that feedback.

1. 360-Degree Instruments.

There are many 360-degree instruments on the market, all designed to give you feedback from your people. Some are better than others. Our own approach is that 360-degree instruments that are customized for the information you want are the only ones worth the investment.

In other words, stay away from off-the-shelf instruments.

You might have the people you need in your organization to develop an effective 360-degree instrument, or maybe you need to look for an outside resource. Your main concern is the instrument's reliability. Does it give you the information you want?

Don't hesitate to come up with your own instrument, in your own words. Sure, your people will know you developed the resource. But they also know they will be giving you the information that shows you how to be an even more effective leader in tough times.

2. Focus Groups.

Another approach is to form focus groups of 6 to 10 people who feel they can openly talk about how you're doing. A focus group can last for an hour or two. Typically, the longer the discussion, the more usable the information. There are three ways to form focus groups.

First you can ask for volunteers. These will often be people who have invested a lot of time and extra energy in the organization. They are ready to give feedback.

Second, you hand-select people, by title, or role, or longevity, or whatever. Just be careful, though, that you're not simply picking people who you think will give you lots of accolades. Yes, we learn by accolades—we learn what we're doing right. But maybe there are some enhancements we can make as leaders, too.

Third, you randomly select people. Put the names of all the people in your unit in a box and have someone pull the names. The pulled names become the people you invite to the focus groups. Randomly selected groups typically provide more usable information than hand-selected groups.

3. Invite Responses to "I wish my leader would just...."

Sure, go ahead, and do what Todd McDonald has done. Distribute pieces of paper to all the people you lead. Ask them to finish the sentence, "I wish my leader would just..." in as many ways as they want. Signing the paper is an option. You're more concerned about the information you get rather than who said it.

As the papers get turned back in, tabulate the findings. The feedback will be helpful as you strive to be an even more effective leader.

Is there a risk to asking this final question, "How am I doing as a leader?" Maybe for your ego. What you will learn, though, is whether or not you're putting in place the contingencies so that people can choose to motivate themselves and be successful.

One of the most powerful leadership skills is the ability to ask people how they want to be managed. It shows confidence, belief in your abilities, and willingness to learn.

It shows that you really want to be a leader in tough times.

Then you can accommodate their styles so that they can be fully productive. As a leader, in tough times or good times, it is easier and more productive for you to accommodate your people's natural strengths than it is to force them to accommodate yours.

* * *

"We are limited, not by our lack of ability, but by our inability to think of ourselves at a point beyond where we are."

(John C. Crystal)

Final Comments

Every organization, every work group, every team, will face tough times. It's not a matter of if, but when. This can be a frightening time. All our hard work is placed in jeopardy. Our futures become uncertain. We lose focus. Momentum is lost. Spirit and energy lag. It's easy to get stuck in the problem.

This is also the time, however, that you, as the leader, can excel. It's up to you to remain confident of the future, show the crisis as temporary, and help people live in the solutions. Leading in tough times isn't easy. It will demand courage on your part to try new things, think in new ways, and challenge "how we do things." But it can be an enlightening and invigorating time.

Once the crisis is past and the tough times behind you, take time to learn why it occurred. Don't let yourself off by blaming the customers, or the employees, or the economy.

Remember: The best time to prepare for the tough times is when things are going well. The guidelines in this book are a good place to start. Set your sights, engage others, and create the life you want to live.

* * *

"The great leaders are like the best conductors—
they reach beyond the notes to reach the magic in the players."

(Blaine Lee, ***The Power Principle***)

References

Aktouf, O. (1996). *Traditional management and beyond: A matter of renewal*. Montreal: Morin.

Belasco, J. A., & Stayler, R. C. (1993). *Flight of the buffalo: Soaring to excellence, learning to let employees lead.* New York: Warner Books, Inc.

Block, P. (2002). *The answer to how is yes*. San Francisco: Berrett-Koehler Publishers.

Buckingham, M., & Coffman, C. (1999). *First, break all the rules: What the world's greatest managers do differently*. New York: Simon & Schuster.

Deems, R. (1995). *Making change work for you!* Des Moines, IA: Provant Media.

Deems, R.S., & Deems, T.A. (2001). Doing downsizing. http://booksurge.com/author.php3? account ID = DEEM00004

Deming, W. (1986). *Out of the crisis*. Cambridge, MA: MIT Press.

Drucker, P.F. (2002). *Managing in the next society*. New York: Truman Talley Books.

Hawley, J. (1993). *Reawakening the spirit in work*. New York: Simon & Schuster.

Kouzes, J.M., & Posner, B.Z. (1995). *The leadership challenge*. San Francisco: Jossey-Bass Publishers.

Langer, E. J. (1989). *Mindfulness*. Reading, MA: Addison-Wesley Publishing Company.

Mitroff, I. I., & Denton, E. A. (1999). *A spiritual audit of corporate America.* San Francisco: Jossey-Bass Publishers.

Pauchant, T.C., and Associates (Eds.) (1995). *In search of meaning: Managing for the health of our organizations, our communities, and the natural world*. San Francisco: Jossey-Bass Publishers.

Robbins, S. P. (2001). *Organizational behavior*. Upper Saddle River, NJ: Prentice-Hall, Inc.

Semler, R. (1993). *Maverick: The success story behind the world's most unusual workplace*. New York: Warner Books, Inc.

Senge, P. M. (1990). *The fifth discipline*. New York: Doubleday.

Senge, P. M. (1999). *The dance of change*. New York: Doubleday.

Wheatley, M. J. (1999). *Leadership and the new science*. San Francisco: Berrett-Koehler Publishers.

Wheatley, M. J. (2002). *Turning to one another: Simple conversations to restore hope to the future*. San Francisco: Berrett-Koehler Publishers.

Interviews/Contributors

Amber, Aldonna, CMC, CSP, President, AMBLER Growth Strategy Consultants, Inc. Hammonton, New Jersey.

Arntsen, Melanie K., Ph.D., Principal, Xamicus. Chandler, Arizona.

Baddeloo, Marty, President, Solutions Kept Simple. West Des Moines, Iowa.

Baum, Herb, CEO and Chair, The Dial Corporation. Scottsdale, Arizona.

Gold, Mike, Manager, Pat's Cleaners. Scottsdale, Arizona.

Jenkins, Natalie, Vice President, Director of Sales, Innova Training & Consulting, Inc. Des Moines, Iowa.

Kastendiek, Steve, Director, Pharmaceutical Contracting McKesson Medication Manager. Minneapolis, Minnesota.

Lepke, Phyllis, Iowa State University Foundation. Ames, Iowa.

McDonald, Gail, Principal, Transition Resources, Inc. Dallas, Texas.

McKnight Latko, Betsy, Principal, Deems McKnight Latko Associates, Inc. Moline, Illinois.

Rambo, Melvin, President, National Travelers Life Company. West Des Moines, Iowa.

Sharpe, Vally M., Principal, Solutions for Organizational Success. Atlanta, Georgia.

Slaughter, David, President, David Slaughter and Associates, Inc. Cibola, Texas.

Taggart, Pete, President, Solutions for Business. Des Moines, Iowa.

Talton, Jon, Business Columnist, *Arizona Republic*. Phoenix, Arizona.

Uribe, Rudy, President, CORE Training Systems. Van Nuys, California.

Van Fossen, Tom, Brokerage Manager, MetLife. Dallas, Texas.

Westheimer, Mary, Founder and Chair, BookZone.com. Phoenix, Arizona.

Index

J

K

L

M

N

O

P

R

S

T

U

V

W

X

About the Authors

Richard S. Deems, Ph.D., is founder and president of Deems Associates, Inc., and its subsidiary, WorkLife Design. He's a nationally recognized expert on organizational change and leadership. Richard has been quoted in *The Wall Street Journal, Federal Times, Executive Excellence,* and even *The Sporting News.* He's the author of nine other books on key management issues including the best selling *Interviewing: More Than a Gut Feeling* and *Making Change Work for You!* A popular presenter, Richard has conducted over 1,000 programs from coast to coast and been interviewed on nearly 100 radio and TV shows.

Richard has held leadership positions in several community-based organizations and served on the graduate faculty at Northern Illinois University and Iowa State University.

Richard received his doctorate from the University of Nebraska–Lincoln, with an emphasis on adult development. His doctoral research focused on developing learning programs for people who had experienced major personal and professional change.

Terri A. Deems, Ph.D., is executive vice president of Deems Associates, Inc., and its subsidiary, WorkLife Design. She's the recipient of the year 2000 International Cutting Edge Award for Research in Human Resource Development, presented by the Academy of Human Resource Development. Her research on personal and organizational change and development has been presented and discussed at numerous national and international conferences.

Terri has held several positions in public and higher education, human resources, and training and development. Like her father, Terri received her doctorate from the University of Nebraska–Lincoln, where her studies and research focused on adult development within the context of work. Terri continues her research on vital, natural workplaces and ways to cultivate more fully human, spirited, work environments.

Terri additionally serves as an adjunct professor instructing courses in organizational behavior, diagnostics and interventions, human relations, training and development, and leadership.